Cambridge English

EMPOWER

STARTER
WORKBOOK
WITH ANSWERS

CW00551901

A1

Rachel Godfrey

Contents

3

1A I'm from Mexico

1 GRAMMAR *be:* I / you / we

a Underline the correct words.

1 How *are you* / *you are*?
2 *I'm* / *I're* fine, thanks.
3 You *not are* / *aren't* in London.
4 *We're* / *We'm* from Spain.
5 Where *am I* / *I am*?
6 **A** Are you OK?
  B No, *I not am* / *I'm not*.
7 **A** Are you a student?
  B Yes, *I am* / *I'm*.
8 **A** Are you from China?
  B No, we *am not* / *aren't*.

b Put the words in the correct order to make sentences and questions.

1 student / a / I'm .
  <u>I'm a student.</u>
2 teachers / aren't / We .
  _____
3 the / from / I'm / not / USA .
  _____
4 OK / Are / you ?
  _____
5 you / are / How ?
  _____
6 London / we / in / Are ?
  _____

2 VOCABULARY Countries

a Find eight countries in the word snake.

BRAZILCHINAITALYJAPANSPAINRUSSIABRITAINTHEUSA

b Complete the sentences with the country names. Use the letters in brackets.

1 Rio de Janeiro is in ___Brazil___. (r a b i l z)
2 Rome and Bologna are in _____. (t i l y a)
3 Tokyo is in _____. (n a j a p)
4 Manchester and London are in _____. (l e g d a n n)
5 Moscow is in _____. (s a r u s i)
6 New York is in _____ (a s h u t e)
7 Barcelona is in _____. (n i s p a)
8 Beijing and Shanghai are in _____. (h a n i c)

3 PRONUNCIATION Long and short sounds

a ▶ 1.1 Listen to the words in the box. What sound do the **marked** letters have? Complete the table.

she	it	is	they're	how	not	from
I'm	Spain	thanks	the	in	hi	

Long sounds	Short sounds
she	it

1 GRAMMAR be: he / she / they

a Complete the sentences with the words in the box.

is she	they aren't	isn't	~~are they~~	are	is	they are

1 Where ___are they___ from?
2 **A** Are they Italian?
  B Yes, _____.
3 **A** _____ they Turkish?
  B No, _____. They're Spanish.
4 **A** _____ from Australia?
  B Yes, she _____.
5 **A** Is he Mexican?
  B No, he _____.

b Complete the conversations with *is, isn't, 's, are, aren't* or *'re*.

Conversation 1
A This [1]___is___ my friend Mia.
B Where [2]_____ she from? [3]_____ she Brazilian?
A No, she [4]_____. She [5]_____ from Spain.

Conversation 2
A Who [6]_____ Bob and Mike? [7]_____ they football players?
B No, they [8]_____. They [9]_____ tennis players.
A [10]_____ they British?
B No, they [11]_____. They [12]_____ American.

▶ **1.2** Listen and check.

2 VOCABULARY Nationalities

a Complete the crossword puzzle.

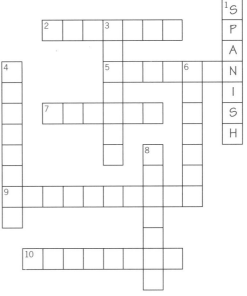

→ **Across**
2 You're from the UK. You're _____.
5 He's from Russia. He's _____.
7 We're from Poland. We're _____.
9 He's from Australia. He's _____.
10 We're from Japan. We're _____.

↓ **Down**
1 They're from Spain. They're ___Spanish___.
3 I'm from Turkey. I'm _____.
4 She's from the USA. She's _____.
6 He's from Italy. He's _____.
8 She's from China. She's _____.

3 PRONUNCIATION
Syllables: nationalities

a ▶ **1.3** Listen to the words in the box. Complete the table.

~~Polish~~ Russian Chinese Italian Brazilian
Turkish Japanese Spanish American Mexican

2 syllables	3 syllables	4 syllables
Polish		

1C Everyday English
Nice to meet you

1 USEFUL LANGUAGE
Meeting and greeting new people

a <u>Underline</u> the correct words to complete the conversations.

Conversation 1 (9 am)

DEBBIE Good ¹*morning / evening*! How are you today?
AYLA I'm not ²*bad / fine*, thanks. And ³*you / are you*?
DEBBIE I'm ⁴*nice / OK*, thanks.

Conversation 2 (3 pm)

JENNY Good ⁵*afternoon / evening*, Dean.
DEAN Hi Jenny. ⁶*She / This* is my friend Becky.
JENNY Hi Becky. How ⁷*you are / are you*?
BECKY I'm good, ⁸*thank / thanks* you.
Nice ⁹*to meet / meet* you.

b ▶1.4 Listen and check.

c Complete the conversation with the words in the box.

and ~~good~~ hello I'm is my
nice thank thanks too

CARLA ¹___Good___ afternoon. ²_____ name's Carla Watkins.
JAMES Hello, ³_____ James Hargreaves.
CARLA ⁴_____ to meet you, James.
JAMES Nice to meet you ⁵_____.
CARLA Oh, Greg! This ⁶_____ James Hargreaves from Electric Blue Technology.
GREG ⁷_____, James! How are you?
JAMES I'm fine, ⁸_____ you. ⁹_____ you?
GREG I'm good, ¹⁰_____.

d ▶1.5 Listen and check.

2 PRONUNCIATION Sentence stress

a ▶1.6 Listen to the sentences. Which words are stressed? Tick (✓) the correct box.

1 a ☑ How <u>are</u> you?
  b ☐ <u>How</u> are you?
2 a ☐ I'm <u>fine</u>, thanks.
  b ☐ I'm fine, <u>thanks</u>.
3 a ☐ So, <u>this</u> is your office.
  b ☐ So, this is <u>your</u> office.
4 a ☐ <u>Good</u> evening!
  b ☐ Good <u>evening</u>!
5 a ☐ I'm Andy <u>and</u> this <u>is</u> Gaston.
  b ☐ I'm <u>Andy</u> and <u>this</u> is <u>Gaston</u>.
6 a ☐ Nice <u>to</u> meet <u>you</u>.
  b ☐ <u>Nice</u> to <u>meet</u> you.

1C Skills for Writing
I'm Turkish.

1 READING

a Read the text and tick (✓) the correct ending for the sentences.

1 Kurt is from …
   a ✓ Germany.
   b ☐ Poland.

2 He's a …
   a ☐ teacher.
   b ☐ student.

3 His teacher …
   a ☐ is British.
   b ☐ isn't British.

4 His friends …
   a ☐ are from Germany.
   b ☐ aren't from Germany.

5 Lia is …
   a ☐ Japanese.
   b ☐ Chinese.

6 Agnessa is from …
   a ☐ Russia.
   b ☐ Poland.

Me and my friends

Hi. My name's Kurt Adler. I'm from Hamburg, in Germany. I'm a student in Warsaw, in Poland. My teacher is from the UK. My friends aren't from Germany or Poland. Lia is from China and Agnessa is from Russia. Ana and Lucas are from Brazil.

2 WRITING SKILLS
Capital letters and full stops

a Underline the correct words.

Hello. ¹*my* / *My* name's ²*kadim* / *Kadim*. I'm ³*Turkish.* / *Turkish* My ⁴*Friends* / *friends* are Justo and ⁵*Emma.* / *Emma* ⁶*They're* / *they're* very nice. Justo is from ⁷*Spain* / *spain* and ⁸*Emma.* / *Emma* is ⁹*American.* / *American*

b Correct the sentences.

1 He's a student He's in your class.
   He's a student. He's in your class.

2 This is diana
   _____

3 My teacher is canadian.
   _____

4 their flat is in london.
   _____

5 I'm from poland.
   _____

6 We're American We're from Seattle.
   _____

3 WRITING

a Write a profile for you. Use Kadim's profile to help you.

Hi! My name's _____
_____
_____
_____
_____
_____
_____
_____
_____
_____
_____
_____
_____
_____

UNIT 1
Reading and listening extension

1 READING

a Read the email and match a–d to the parts of the email 1–4.

a ☐ saying goodbye
b ☐ Mark's new job
c ☐ greeting
d ☐ people in Mark's office

b Read the email again. Are the sentences true or false?

1 Jerry is in Australia.
2 Mark is in Brisbane.
3 Tony is Australian.
4 Tony and Janine are married.
5 Janine is a teacher.
6 Martin is from England.
7 Yoko is from Japan.
8 Yoko is at home in the afternoon.

c Write an email to a friend about your new English class. Remember to say:

• where your class is
• who your teacher is and where he or she is from
• who the students are and where they are from.

1 Hi Jerry,

How are you? How is England?

2 I'm fine. My new job in Australia is good. The office is in Brisbane and it's in the centre of the city. Brisbane is great! ☺

3 I'm in an office with three people: Tony, Martin and Yoko. Our office manager is Tony. He's not Australian. He's from a small town in the USA, but he's married to an Australian woman. Her name's Janine and she's a teacher in a language school. Martin is Australian. He's from Sydney, but his home is Brisbane now. Yoko is Japanese. She's from Osaka. She's in the office from 8 am to 1 pm and she's a student at an English school in the afternoon.

4 Say hello to all my friends in England!

Bye for now,

Mark

Review

1 GRAMMAR

Correct the mistakes.

1 Janka aren't German. She's Polish.
   Janka isn't German. She's Polish.
2 **A** Where you are?
   B I'm in Barcelona.
3 I not am a student. I'm a teacher.
4 **A** And who this is?
   B This is Anton.
5 These are my friends. They American.
6 What your name?
7 We not Italian. We're Mexican.
8 Where Sue is from?

2 VOCABULARY

Tick (✓) the sentences that are correct. Correct the mistakes.

1 ☐ They're from UK.
   They're from the UK.
2 ☐ She's Mexican.
3 ☐ He's from the Russia.
4 ☐ She's from the USA.
5 ☐ We're Brasilian.
6 ☐ Are you Spainish?
7 ☐ I'm Japanese.
8 ☐ He's from Poland.

2 LISTENING

a ▶ **1.7** Listen to the conversation. Tick (✓) the countries you hear.

Brazil	☐	Russia	☐
China	☐	Turkey	☐
England	☐	Scotland	✓
Japan	☐	the USA	✓

b ▶ **1.7** Listen again and underline the correct words.

1 It is *morning* / *evening*.
2 Anne and Tom are *at home* / *at work*.
3 *Anne* / *Tom* is a new teacher.
4 Edinburgh is a city in *Scotland* / *England*.
5 Anne is from *London* / *Manchester*.
6 Tom's class is *1A* / *1B*.
7 Daniela is a *Brazilian* / *Russian* student.
8 Alim and Fehim are *Spanish* / *Turkish*.

c Complete the conversation with your own ideas.

A Good morning.
B Hi. Are you new?
A Yes, I am. My name's _____.
B It's nice to meet you. I'm _____.
A Nice to meet you too.
B Where are you from?
A _____, in _____.
B Really? _____'s a nice city.

⬢ REVIEW YOUR PROGRESS

Look again at Review your progress on p.14 of the Student's Book. How well can you do these things now?

3 = very well   2 = well   1 = not so well

I CAN ...

say my name and country	☐
talk about people I know	☐
meet and greet new people.	☐

9

1 GRAMMAR be: it's / it isn't

a Underline the correct words.

1 This is Santiago. *It's* / *He's* a big city in Chile.
2 This is my home. *It's* / *They're* a small flat.
3 Nina's Russian. *It's* / *She's* from Vyborg.
4 The houses are new. *It isn't* / *They aren't* very big.
5 Adel is German. *He's* / *It's* from Berlin.
6 **A** Is Barcelona a small city?
  B No, it *isn't* / *not*.
7 I'm from Göreme. *It's* / *She's* a town in Turkey.
8 **A** Are the flats in the old part of town?
  B Yes, *they are* / *it is*.

2 GRAMMAR Possessive adjectives

a Write the correct possessive adjective. Use the pronoun in brackets to help you.

1 We're from London. _____Our_____ (we) house is very old.
2 **A** What's _____ (you) name?
  B I'm Celine. I'm from Paris.
3 Where's John? This is _____ (he) book.
4 **A** They're from Moscow.
  B What are _____ (they) names?
5 I'm Bruno. I'm from Italy but _____ (I) mother is English.
6 This is my friend. She's from China and _____ (she) name is Jia.

3 VOCABULARY Common adjectives

a Match the **marked** words with the opposite adjectives a–g.

1 [f] It's a **big** village.   a bad
2 [ ] This book is **boring**.   b easy
3 [ ] He's a very **good** football player!   c interesting
4 [ ] Why are they **happy**?   d old
5 [ ] This vocabulary is **difficult**.   e sad
6 [ ] Is your computer **new**?   f small
7 [ ] You're **right**.   g wrong

b Look at the pictures and complete the adjectives.

1 f u n n y   2 r _ _ _ _   3 d _ _ _ _ _ _ t

4 _ oo _   5 h _ _ _ y   6 b _ a _ _ _ _ l

7 e _ _ y   8 b _ _ _ g   9 i _ _ _ _ _ t _ _

4 PRONUNCIATION
Sound and spelling: /h/

a ▶ 2.1 Listen to the words in the box. Do they have the /h/ sound? Complete the table.

| ~~this~~ he she China his her hello |
| what who happy that phone |

/h/ sound	No /h/ sound
	this

2B Do you have a phone?

1 GRAMMAR Plural nouns

a Underline the correct spelling.

1. citys / <u>cities</u>
2. ticketes / tickets
3. watches / watchs
4. bottle of waters / bottle of water
5. knifes / knives
6. countries / countrys
7. boys / boyes
8. babies / babys
9. villages / villagees
10. keys / keyes

2 GRAMMAR have

a Put the words in the correct order to complete the conversation.

JESSICA	Oh no!
TIMO	What is it?
JESSICA	My bag! It's at home!
TIMO	Oh no. [1]pen / you / have / a / do ?
	<u>Do you have a pen?</u>
JESSICA	No, I don't!
TIMO	Here you are. [2]pens / two / I / have .
	_____
JESSICA	Thanks.
TIMO	And [3]you / a / dictionary / do / have ?
	_____
JESSICA	Yes, [4]dictionary / have / a / I .
	_____
TIMO	Good.
JESSICA	Timo, [5]have / you / of / bottle / do / a / water ?
	_____
TIMO	No, I don't. Sorry. But [6]I / apple / an / have !
	_____
JESSICA	No thanks, Timo!

3 VOCABULARY Common objects 1

a Look at the picture. Write the words.

1. a _____*bag*_____
2. a b _____
3. k _____
4. an u _____
5. a p _____
6. a _____ of water

4 VOCABULARY Numbers 1

a ▶2.2 Listen and write the correct number.

1. I have _____*eighty*_____ books.
2. _____ apples, please.
3. I have _____ bags.
4. _____ eggs, please.
5. Do you have _____ tickets?
6. _____ bottles of water, please.

5 PRONUNCIATION
Sound and spelling: /s/, /z/ and /ɪz/

a ▶2.3 Listen to the words in the box. Is the final sound /s/, /z/ or /ɪz/? Complete the table.

knives villages students newspapers
tickets books watches bottles houses

Sound 1 /s/	Sound 2 /z/	Sound 3 /ɪz/
	knives	

2C Everyday English
What's your address?

1 USEFUL LANGUAGE
Asking for and giving personal information

a Complete the questions. Use the letters in brackets.

1 What's your __address__? (s d a d r e s)
2 How do you _____ that? (l s p l e)
3 What's your _____ _____?
   (onmenupberh)
4 What's your _____ _____?
   (s e d m d a e i l a r s)
5 What's your _____ _____?
   (t i n r s a f e m)

b Complete the conversation with the questions in the box.

> How do you spell that?
> What's your phone number?
> What's your address?
> ~~What's your surname?~~

A ¹What's your surname? _____
B It's Milner.
A ² _____
B M-I-L-N-E-R.
A ³ _____
B It's 39 Oak Street, Brighton.
A ⁴ _____
B It's 07896 7421019.

c ▶2.4 Listen and check.

d Complete the conversation.

A What's your ¹ __surname__ ?
B ² _____ Gibbins.
A ³ _____ do you spell that?
B G-I-B-B-I-N-S.
A ⁴ _____ your phone number?
B ⁵ _____ 09745 833081.
A What's your email ⁶ _____?
B ⁷ _____ alice888@zipmail.com.

e ▶2.5 Listen and check.

2 PRONUNCIATION Tone in questions

a ▶2.6 Listen to the questions. Does the tone go up (↗) or down (↘) at the end? Tick the correct box.

	↗	↘
1 How are you?		✓
2 Is it a village?		
3 What's your surname?		
4 What's your address?		
5 Can you spell that?		
6 What's the spelling?		
7 Are you from a big city?		
8 Is this your phone?		
9 Where are you from?		
10 What's your email address?		

1 READING

a Read the information. Complete the form with the words in the box.

Stewart	American	Office
Gem	~~Kerry~~	745	9178

MONTY'S BOOK COMPANY

OUR PEOPLE

 Hi. My name's Kerry Stewart. I'm from the USA. Perth's a great city and I'm very happy here! My office is in the Gem Building in White Street. I'm in Room 745 with Kadim Baydar and Sandro Alessi. Our office phone number is 8969. My email address is kerryoz9178@powermail.com.

First name:	[1] _Kerry_
Surname:	[2] _____
Nationality:	[3] _____
Home address:	Flat 2, 28 Village Avenue, Perth
Mobile phone number:	07756 435028
Office address:	Room [4] _____, The [5] _____ Building, White Street, Perth
[6] _____ phone number:	8969
Email address:	kerryoz [7] _____@powermail.com

2 WRITING SKILLS
The alphabet and spelling

a Underline the letter with the different sound.

1 A   J   K   <u>R</u>
2 B   C   D   F
3 M   N   G   Z
4 O   Q   U   W
5 I   X   Y

b Correct the spelling.

1 bottel   _bottle_
2 spel   _____
3 eesy   _____
4 fone   _____
5 addres   _____
6 villige   _____
7 hapy   _____
8 nashionality _____
9 offis   _____
10 emale   _____

3 WRITING

a Complete the form with information about you.

First name:	_____
Surname:	_____
Nationality:	_____
Home address:	_____
	_____
Phone number:	_____
Email:	_____

UNIT 2
Reading and listening extension

1 READING

a Read the text. Tick (✓) the correct summary 1–4.

1 ☐ Emily and Mark are married. They are managers in Hull. They have a house in a village near Hull.

2 ☐ Emily and Mark are married. They have a house in Hull. Mark is a manager in a small town near Hull.

3 ☐ Emily and Mark have a house in Hull. They are receptionists in a big office in Hull.

4 ☐ Mark is a receptionist in Hull. He is married to Emily. They have a house in a town near Hull.

b Read the text again. Tick (✓) the correct answer.

1 Is Hull a small town?
   a ☐ Yes, it is.
   b ✓ No, it isn't.

2 Is Hull old?
   a ☐ Yes, it is.
   b ☐ No, it isn't.

3 Is it a boring place?
   a ☐ Yes, it is.
   b ☐ No, it isn't.

4 Is Mark's office near an airport?
   a ☐ Yes, it is.
   b ☐ No, it isn't.

5 Is Brough a big town?
   a ☐ Yes, it is.
   b ☐ No, it isn't.

6 Is Emily and Mark's house new?
   a ☐ Yes, it is.
   b ☐ No, it isn't.

7 Is their house near a supermarket?
   a ☐ Yes, it is.
   b ☐ No, it isn't.

8 Is Mark happy?
   a ☐ Yes, he is.
   b ☐ No, he isn't.

ABOUT

My name is Mark Smith and I work in Hull in England. Hull is a big city with 260,000 people. It's old and it has an interesting history. I'm a receptionist in an office in the centre of Hull. My office is in a nice part of the city. It's near a big park.

My home isn't in Hull, it's in Brough. Brough is a small town near Hull with 7,000 people. It's a nice town with a park, two supermarkets and a hotel. I'm married to Emily and we have two children.

Our house is in the centre of Brough. It's a small house and it's new. It isn't near the park, but it is near one of the supermarkets. I'm very happy here. I have a lot of friends in Brough and in Hull, and my job isn't boring!

c Write about your home. Think about these questions:

- Where is your home?
- Is your home big or small? Is it old or new?
- Is your home in a town, a city or a village?
- Is your town, city or village interesting or boring?
- What is near your home?

2 LISTENING

a  **2.7** Listen. Complete the sentences with the words in the box.

---
one desk   two desks   three desks
---

1 Speaker 1, Darren, has _____.
2 Speaker 2, Paula, has _____.
3 Speaker 3, Jamie, has _____.

b **2.7** Listen again. Match pictures a–c to speakers 1–3.

1 ☐ Darren   2 ☐ Paula   3 ☐ Jamie

(a)

(b)

(c)

c **2.7** Listen again. What does each person have on their desk? Complete the table with the words in the box.

---
apple   glass of water   keys   handbag   knife
laptop   newspaper   ~~phone~~   umbrella

Speaker 1: Darren	Speaker 2: Paula	Speaker 3: Jamie
phone		

Write about your desk. Use the Audioscript on p.82 to help you. Think about these questions:

- Where is your desk?
- Is your desk old or new?
- Is your desk big or small?
- What is on your desk?
- What isn't on your desk?

Review

1 GRAMMAR

Correct the mistakes.

1 Is this you computer?
   Is this your computer?
2 I have three watch.
3 They're a beautiful village.
4 Beijing is a big cities.
5 This is Kira and Paul and this is they're house.
6 My flat is in an old part of town. They're very small.
7 Where's Anna? This is she's bag.
8 Where are the knifes?

2 VOCABULARY

Correct the spelling.

1 eigt tickets
   eight tickets
2 smal bottles of water
3 thirten flats
4 an intresting city
5 twelv phones
6 beatiful houses
7 an old umbrela
8 funy books

3A Do you like fish?

1 GRAMMAR
Present simple: I / you / we / they

a Underline the correct words.

1 We *fruit eat* / *eat fruit* every day.
2 *Do you eat* / *You eat* bread?
3 They *no eat* / *don't eat* eggs.
4 **A** Do you like vegetables?
  B No, *don't* / *I don't*.
5 *Like you* / *Do you like* fish?
6 **A** Do you like meat?
  B No, we *don't like* / *don't*.
7 I *don't like* / *not like* rice.
8 **A** Do you like fruit?
  B Yes, I *do* / *like*.

b ▶**3.1** Listen and check.

c Complete the conversation with the words in the box.

do	like	don't	you eat	do you	~~like meat~~	don't eat

DUNCAN Mmm! I ¹ _like meat_ ! I eat meat every day!
RAJIT Really? I ² _____ meat.
DUNCAN Oh, you don't eat meat. Do ³ _____ fish?
RAJIT No, I ⁴ _____.
DUNCAN ⁵ _____ eat eggs?
RAJIT Yes, I ⁶ _____. I ⁷ _____ eggs.

d ▶**3.2** Listen and check.

2 VOCABULARY Food 1

a Write the words under the pictures.

meat	vegetables	~~fish~~	milk	tea	cola
bread	rice	coffee	fruit juice	eggs	fruit

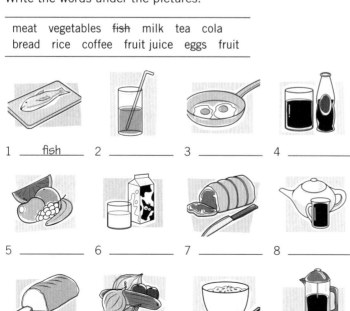

1 _fish_   2 _____   3 _____   4 _____

5 _____   6 _____   7 _____   8 _____

9 _____ 10 _____ 11 _____ 12 _____

b Complete the crossword puzzle.

→ **Across**

2 C_____ is a drink. It's from Brazil, Colombia and other countries.
6 V_____ are food. They're good for you.
7 W_____ is a drink. It's good for you.
10 E_____ are food from chickens.
11 C_____ is a drink. It isn't very good for you!

↓ **Down**

1 Lots of people eat b<u>read</u>_____ every day.
3 F_____ juice is a drink.
4 F_____ is food. It's an animal in the sea.
5 M_____ is food from animals.
8 R_____ is food. It's from China, India and other countries.
9 Lots of people drink t_____ every day.

3 PRONUNCIATION Sound and spelling: /iː/, /ɪ/ and /aɪ/

a ▶**3.3** Listen to the words in the box. What sound do the **marked** letters have? Complete the table.

~~my~~	tea	this	rice	milk	is
I	we	like	Italy	meat	key

Sound 1 /iː/ (e.g. *be*)	Sound 2 /ɪ/ (e.g. *it*)	Sound 3 /aɪ/ (e.g. *by*)
		my

3B I always have dinner early

1 GRAMMAR Adverbs of frequency

a Underline the correct words.

1 We *sometimes have* / *have sometimes* eggs for breakfast.
2 I *eat never* / *never eat* biscuits at work.
3 You *have usually* / *usually have* a sandwich for lunch.
4 They *have always* / *always have* cake at the weekend.
5 I *sometimes eat* / *eat sometimes* an apple at lunchtime.
6 I *have never* / *never have* dinner at 7:00.

b Look at the table and complete the sentences.
Use *always*, *usually*, *sometimes* or *never* and the
present simple of the verbs in brackets.

1 I ___never eat___ fish. (eat)
2 I _____ lunch in a café. (eat)
3 I _____ rice for lunch. (eat)
4 I _____ lunch at work. (have)
5 I _____ cereal for breakfast. (have)
6 I _____ dinner at home. (have)

Food and me

eat fish	x
eat lunch in a café	every day
eat rice for lunch	on Wednesdays and Saturdays
have lunch at work	x
have cereal for breakfast	on Mondays, Tuesdays, Wednesdays, Thursdays and Fridays
have dinner at home	every day

2 VOCABULARY Food 2

a Underline the correct words to complete the
conversations.

1 **A** What fruit do you like?
   B Apples and *sandwiches* / *potatoes* / *bananas*.
2 **A** Would you like *a biscuit* / *a butter* / *an orange* with your
      coffee?
   B No thanks.
3 **A** A *sandwich* / *pizza* / *tomato* is a vegetable.
   B No, it isn't. It's a fruit!
4 **A** We have bread, butter and eggs.
   B Good! *An egg sandwich* / *A cake* / *An apple* for me,
      please.
5 **A** A cheese and tomato *apple* / *pizza* / *ice cream*, please.
   B Certainly.
6 **A** Is this fruit juice?
   B Yes, it's *cake* / *orange* / *cheese* juice.

▶ 3.4 Listen and check.

3 VOCABULARY Time

a Look at the clocks and complete the times. Use the
words in the box.

eleven half o'clock past quarter (x2) ten to

1 eight *o'clock* _____
2 half past _____

3 quarter _____ seven
4 _____ to one

5 _____ o'clock
6 quarter _____ six

7 _____ past one
8 _____ past one

b ▶ 3.5 Listen and check.

4 PRONUNCIATION
Sound and spelling: /ɑː/ and /ɔː/

a ▶ 3.6 Listen to the words in the box. What sound do
the **marked** letters have? Complete the table.

~~morning~~ afternoon half past always four water class banana small

Sound 1 /ɑː/ (e.g. *car*)	Sound 2 /ɔː/ (e.g. *your*)
	morning

1 USEFUL LANGUAGE
Ordering and paying in a café

a Complete the expressions with the words in the box.

cola   sandwich   ~~coffee~~   are   course   cake

1 a cup of _____coffee_____
2 a piece of _____
3 here you _____
4 a glass of _____
5 a cheese _____
6 of _____

b Complete the conversation with the sentences in the box.

No, thanks.
Can I have a cup of coffee, please?
OK. Thank you very much.
~~Hello. I'd like a piece of fruit cake, please.~~

WAITRESS	Good morning.
NANCY	¹Hello. I'd like a piece of fruit cake, please.
WAITRESS	Certainly. And to drink?
NANCY	²_____
WAITRESS	Of course. With milk?
NANCY	³_____
WAITRESS	Here you are. That's £6.50, please.
NANCY	⁴_____
WAITRESS	Thank you.

c ▶ 3.7 Listen and check.

d <u>Underline</u> the correct words to complete the conversation.

WAITER	Good afternoon.
SAM	Hello. ¹*I have / I'd like* a cup of tea, please.
WAITER	Certainly. And to ²*eat / drink*?
SAM	³*I'd like / I like* a cheese sandwich, please.
WAITER	With tomato?
SAM	No, thanks. And ⁴*I'd / can I* have some chocolate cake and a glass ⁵*water / of water* too, please?
WAITER	Of course! That's £11, please.
SAM	OK. Here ⁶*you are / are you*.
WAITER	Thank you.

e ▶ 3.8 Listen and check.

2 PRONUNCIATION   Sentence stress

a ▶ 3.9 Listen to the sentences. Which words are stressed? Tick (✓) the correct box.

1 a ☐ a <u>piece</u> of pizza
  b ✓ a <u>piece</u> of <u>pizza</u>

2 a ☐ <u>a</u> cup <u>of</u> coffee
  b ☐ a <u>cup</u> of <u>coffee</u>

3 a ☐ a <u>glass</u> of <u>water</u>
  b ☐ <u>a</u> glass of water

4 a ☐ <u>a</u> piece of <u>cheese</u>
  b ☐ a <u>piece</u> of <u>cheese</u>

5 a ☐ a <u>glass</u> of <u>fruit</u> juice
  b ☐ a glass <u>of</u> fruit <u>juice</u>

6 a ☐ a <u>cup</u> of <u>tea</u>
  b ☐ <u>a</u> cup of <u>tea</u>

7 a ☐ a glass <u>of</u> <u>milk</u>
  b ☐ a <u>glass</u> of <u>milk</u>

8 a ☐ a <u>piece</u> of <u>chocolate</u> <u>cake</u>
  b ☐ a piece <u>of</u> chocolate <u>cake</u>

3C Skills for Writing
I'm in a café

1 READING

a Read the text messages. Are the sentences true or false?

1 Tony's with a friend from Poland.
2 Kaspar's funny.
3 Esther's at work.
4 Felix and Esther are students.
5 Omar likes his work.
6 Clara's at work.

 Hi Lisa, I'm in a café with Kaspar. He's my new friend. He's Polish. He's very funny! Talk soon, Tony

 Hi Misha, I'm in a restaurant with Felix. He's a student in my class. We like our new teacher very much. She's from Spain. See you later, Esther

 Hi Clara, I'm at work. It's boring! Where are you? Why aren't you here? Talk to you soon, Omar

2 WRITING SKILLS Contractions

a Write the full form of the contractions.

1 I'm   I am
2 She isn't   _____
3 He's   _____
4 We don't   _____
5 They aren't _____
6 It's   _____

b Complete the text messages with the words in brackets. Use contractions.

1 Hi Emre, ___I'm___ (I am) in a café with Julio and Marta. _____ (they are) really nice! See you later, Ana

2 Hi Freda, _____ (we are) at the restaurant. _____ (You are not) here! Where are you? Tilde

3 Hi Danny, I _____ (do not) like work! It's boring! Kira

4 Hi Mel, _____ (we are) in Rome. _____ (It is) a beautiful city! Talk later, Linda

5 Hi Greg, _____ (I am) at work with Yuri. _____ (He is not) very happy. See you later, Sol

6 Hi Matt, _____ (I am not) happy today. My teacher is boring. Fay

3 WRITING

a Write a text message to a friend. Think about these questions:

- Where are you?
- Are you at work?
- Who are you with?

Hi

1 READING

a Read about meals in Italy. <u>Underline</u> the correct words to complete the sentences.

1 In Italy, people *eat* / *don't eat* a lot of fruit and vegetables.
2 Italians drink a lot of *tea* / *coffee*.
3 They *like* / *don't like* meat and fish.
4 They usually have *three* / *four* meals every day.
5 Italian people *have* / *don't have* pasta every day.
6 For a lot of people, the big meal is in the *afternoon* / *evening*.

b Read the text again. Are the sentences true or false?

1 Breakfast is at 9:00.
2 Maria and her family have coffee and cereal for breakfast.
3 On work days, Maria and her friends have lunch in the office.
4 At weekends, Maria has lunch with her family.
5 A *panino* is a pizza.
6 Dinner is at 8:30.
7 They sometimes have pasta for dinner.
8 They often have cake in the morning.

c Write about the meals you have every day. Think about these questions:

- How many meals do you have?
- What time do you have your meals?
- What do you usually have for breakfast, lunch and dinner?

Meals in ITALY

My name is Maria and I'm Italian. In Italy, people eat different foods. We like pasta and pizza, but we don't eat them every day. We like a lot of different meat and fish. And we eat a lot of fruit and vegetables.

In my family, we have three meals a day. Breakfast is at eight o'clock. We eat *fette biscottate*, a type of breakfast bread, and have coffee with milk. Italian people usually drink a lot of coffee!

On work days, my lunch is always at one o'clock. I never have lunch in my office. I usually have a *panino* (that's a sandwich) or a slice of pizza with my friends in a café near the office. At the weekend I have lunch at home with my family.

Dinner is the big meal of the day for a lot of Italians. In my family, we always have dinner at half past eight. We have rice or pasta, then fish with vegetables. We don't eat a lot of meat. After dinner, we usually have fruit and coffee, but at the weekend we sometimes have cake.

2 LISTENING

a ▶ **3.10** Listen to the conversation. Tick (✓) the food and drink words you hear.

cheese	✓	banana	☐
meat	☐	ice cream	☐
egg	☐	tea	☐
fish	☐	fruit juice	☐
chocolate	☐	water	☐

b ▶ **3.10** Listen again. Tick (✓) who says the sentences.

	John	Anna
1 I never eat cheese.	✓	
2 Do you like eggs?		
3 I like eggs.		
4 I eat a lot of tomatoes.		
5 I don't eat a lot of chocolate.		
6 I usually drink tea.		
7 I don't like hot drinks.		
8 I always have orange juice for breakfast.		

c Write about food and drinks you like and don't like. Use these expressions:

- I eat a lot of …
- I don't drink a lot of …
- I never eat …
- I always drink …

⊙ Review

1 GRAMMAR

Tick (✓) the sentences that are correct. Correct the mistakes.

1 ☑ Do you like eggs?
2 ☐ I never eat cake.
3 ☐ We have sometimes pizza.
4 ☐ They don't like ice cream.
5 ☐ I like fruit.
6 ☐ I not like cheese.
7 ☐ You like meat?
8 ☐ They eat usually pizza for lunch.

2 VOCABULARY

Tick (✓) the sentences that are correct. Correct the mistakes.

1 ☐ I like vegtables.
   I like *vegetables*.
2 ☐ We have lunch at 12:45 pm.
3 ☐ We eat rise for lunch every day.
4 ☐ Do you have an apple?
5 ☐ I never eat biscits.
6 ☐ We have a breakfast at 7:30 am.
7 ☐ I don't like cake.
8 ☐ That sanwich is very big!

⟳ REVIEW YOUR PROGRESS

Look again at Review your progress on p.14 of the Student's Book. How well can you do these things now?
3 = very well   2 = well   1 = not so well

I CAN …

say what I eat and drink	☐
talk about food and meals	☐
order and pay in a café.	☐

4A What do you study?

1 GRAMMAR
Present simple: Wh- questions

a Put the words in the correct order to make questions.

1 live / where / do / you ?
Where do you live?

2 's / flat / your / where ?
_____

3 lunch / eat / what / for / you / do ?
_____

4 are / names / their / what ?
_____

5 do / study / where / you ?
_____

6 at / when / she / work / 's ?
_____

b Underline the correct words.

1 What time *is / are / do* you go to the gym?
2 What languages *is / are / do* you speak?
3 What *is / are / do* the time?
4 When *is / are / do* you meet your friends?
5 Where *is / are / do* you from?
6 Where *is / are / do* the university?
7 When *is / are / do* you at home?
8 What *is / are / do* you study?

2 VOCABULARY Common verbs

a Tick (✓) the correct words to complete the sentences.

1 You _____ Spanish.
  a ☐ live   b ✓ speak   c ☐ meet

2 We _____ Japanese.
  a ☐ meet   b ☐ study   c ☐ work

3 I _____ my friends every day.
  a ☐ meet   b ☐ go   c ☐ work

4 We _____ football.
  a ☐ go   b ☐ play   c ☐ speak

5 I _____ at an English language school.
  a ☐ go   b ☐ live   c ☐ teach

6 We _____ to the gym every day.
  a ☐ go   b ☐ study   c ☐ teach

b Complete the crossword puzzle.

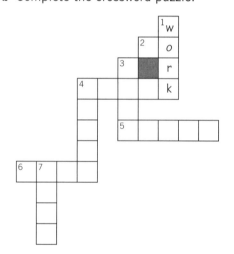

→ **Across**

2 They _____ to school every day.
4 I _____ English, German and Russian.
5 I _____ young children in a small school.
6 We _____ tennis every day.

↓ **Down**

1 I ___*work*___ in a factory.
3 I _____ my friends after school.
4 We _____ English at a language school.
7 You _____ in a big house.

3 PRONUNCIATION Sentence stress

a ▶️ 4.1 Listen to the sentences and underline the stressed words.

1 Where do you live?
2 Do you speak French?
3 Do you work in a factory?
4 What do you study?
5 Do you go to the gym?
6 When do you have lunch?

4B She has a sister and a brother

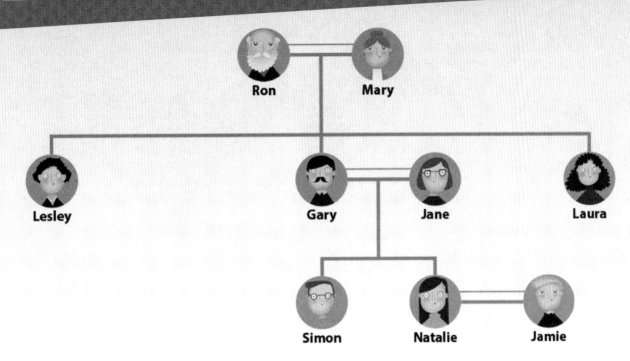

Ron   Mary

Lesley   Gary   Jane   Laura

Simon   Natalie   Jamie

1 GRAMMAR
Present simple: *he / she / it* positive

a Underline the correct words.

1 Pablo *haves* / *has* an international family.
2 My dad *teachs* / *teaches* at the university.
3 Debbie *lives* / *livs* in a big house.
4 Sandro *works* / *workes* in an office.
5 My brother *studys* / *studies* at high school.
6 Lisa *plays* / *playes* the guitar.
7 Ryan *speakes* / *speaks* Chinese.
8 My mum *goes* / *gos* to the gym every day.

b Complete the sentences with the correct form of the verbs in brackets.

1 Dean ____likes____ tennis and football. (like)
2 My sister _____ to the cinema every weekend. (go)
3 Jack _____ Italian at university. (study)
4 Mandy _____ a sister and two brothers. (have)
5 My brother _____ cola every day. (drink)
6 My mum _____ young children. (teach)
7 William _____ at home. (work)
8 My friend Sonya _____ in Berlin. (live)

2 VOCABULARY Numbers 2

a Write the numbers in words.

51	_fifty-one_
27	_____
45	_____
89	_____
34	_____
98	_____
66	_____
100	_____
72	_____

3 VOCABULARY Family and people

a Look at the family tree. Complete the sentences with the words in the box.

brother	daughter	father	~~husband~~
mother	parents	sister	son	wife

1 Gary is Jane's ____husband____.
2 Gary is Natalie's _____.
3 Jane is Simon's _____.
4 Ron and Mary are Laura's _____.
5 Simon is Natalie's _____.
6 Lesley is Ron's _____.
7 Simon is Gary's _____.
8 Natalie is Jamie's _____.
9 Laura is Lesley's _____.

4 PRONUNCIATION
Sound and spelling: /ð/

a ▶4.2 Listen and tick (✓) the words that have the /ð/ sound.

1 she ☐
2 that ☐
3 right ☐
4 father ☐
5 mother ☐
6 three ☐
7 they ☐
8 the ☐
9 eight ☐
10 brother ☐

1 USEFUL LANGUAGE
Asking and talking about photos

a Underline the correct words to complete the conversation.

CATH ¹*Can I see / Do you have* photos of your home?
AMY Yes, ²*I do / do*.
CATH ³*Can I see / This is* them?
AMY Sure. ⁴*This is / This* my flat.
CATH ⁵*Who does / Who's* this?
AMY My brother Harry.
CATH ⁶*Great / Is great* photo!
AMY Thanks. Here's another picture of my flat.
CATH ⁷*It / It's* really nice.

b ▶️**4.3** Listen and check.

c Put the conversation in the correct order.

	JENNY	Nice picture!
	JENNY	They're lovely! Thank you.
1	JENNY	Do you have photos of your family?
	JENNY	Can I see them?
	SEAN	And this is .me with my mum and my sister.
	SEAN	Sure. This is my dad and my brother.
	SEAN	Yes, I do.

d ▶️**4.4** Listen and check.

2 PRONUNCIATION
Sound and spelling: /tʃ/ and /dʒ/

a ▶️**4.5** Listen to the words in the box. What sound do the **marked** letters have? Complete the table.

~~orange~~ question cheap page child Japan
Germany manager picture watch

Sound 1 /tʃ/ (e.g. lunch)	Sound 2 /dʒ/ (e.g. change)
	orange

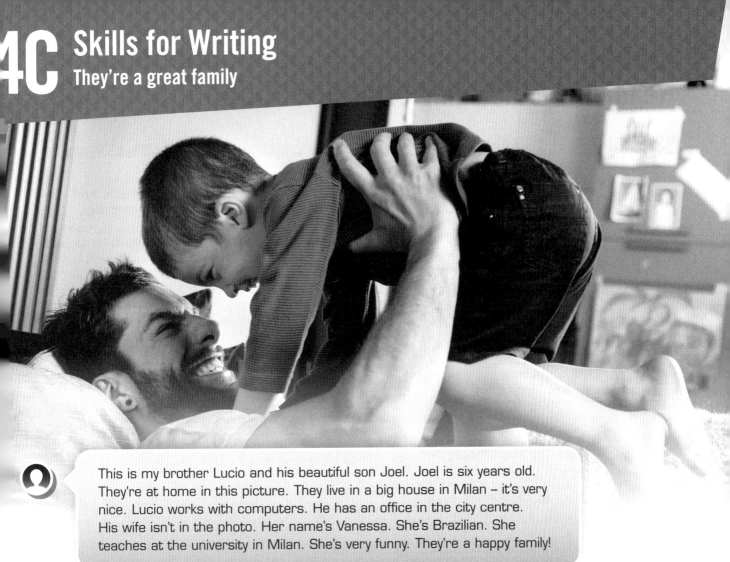

> This is my brother Lucio and his beautiful son Joel. Joel is six years old. They're at home in this picture. They live in a big house in Milan – it's very nice. Lucio works with computers. He has an office in the city centre. His wife isn't in the photo. Her name's Vanessa. She's Brazilian. She teaches at the university in Milan. She's very funny. They're a happy family!

1 READING

a Read about the photo. <u>Underline</u> the correct answers.

1 Joel is *six* / *thirty-six*.
2 Lucio and Joel have a *small* / *big* home.
3 They live in *Italy* / *Brazil*.
4 Lucio works with *children* / *computers*.
5 Lucio *is* / *isn't* married.
6 Vanessa is a university *teacher* / *student*.
7 She *lives in* / *is from* Brazil.
8 Vanessa, Lucio and Joel *are* / *aren't* happy.

2 WRITING SKILLS Word order

a Tick (✓) the correct sentences.

1 a ✓ We don't work.
  b ☐ We work don't.

2 a ☐ We have a big meal in the evening.
  b ☐ We have in the evening a big meal.

3 a ☐ They don't have a pencil in their bag.
  b ☐ They don't have in their bag a pencil.

4 a ☐ We play at school football.
  b ☐ We play football at school.

5 a ☐ I like in my tea sugar.
  b ☐ I like sugar in my tea.

6 a ☐ She doesn't in London work.
  b ☐ She doesn't work in London.

b Put the words in the correct order to make sentences.

1 his daughters / this / is / my friend / with .
<u>This is my friend with his daughters.</u>

2 family / lovely / a / they're .
_____

3 here / I / live / don't .
_____

4 Ruben and Cara / these / children / are / my .
_____

5 a / Mexico / have / flat / small / I / City / in .
_____

6 English / at / sister / my / university / studies .
_____

3 WRITING

a Write a caption for a favourite photo of you with your friends or family. Remember to give information about:

• who the people are
• where they are
• what job or studies they do.

_____
_____

UNIT 4
Reading and listening extension

1 READING

a Read the email and match the people 1–6 to the places a–f.

1 [e] Daniel   a Warsaw
2 [   ] Eileen   b Moscow
3 [   ] Elizabetta   c Edinburgh
4 [   ] Greg and Maria   d San Francisco
5 [   ] Jon   e Mexico City
6 [   ] Tom   f Washington

b Read the email again. Complete the family tree with the names in the box.

Jeff   Anna   Olga   ~~Elizabetta~~
Maria   Daniel   Greg   Tom

Hi Eileen,

Thanks for your email. I love the photos of your family. You have a big family! My family is small. Here's a new photo of us on holiday.

I'm with my husband, Greg, our daughter, Linda, and our son, Jeff. My parents, Tom and Elizabetta, are in the photo, too. My dad is American. He's from San Francisco, but my mother comes from Warsaw in Poland. Greg and I live in Washington with our children. Greg works in an office and I'm a teacher (as you know). Greg's parents live in Washington, too, so we see them one or two days a week, but my mum and dad are in California. We usually have holidays with them.

I have two brothers, Daniel and Jon. They aren't in the photo. Daniel is an English teacher in Mexico City and Jon lives in Moscow. Jon's wife, Anna, is Russian and they have a daughter. Her name's Olga. We sometimes see them in the holidays. Olga is five and she speaks Russian and English very well.

Write soon and tell me more about your life in Edinburgh.

Maria

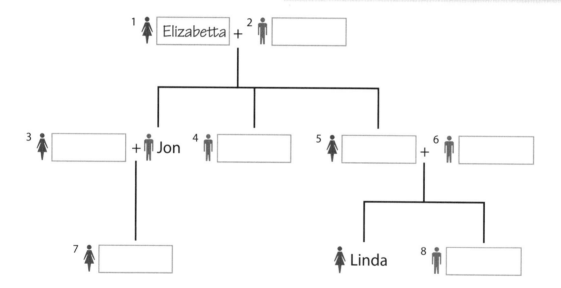

c Draw your family tree and write about the people in your family. Say:

- their names and ages
- what they do (job or studies)
- where they live.

Review

1 GRAMMAR

Correct the mistakes.

1 Where you study?
   Where do you study?
2 He work in Barcelona.
3 She haves two brothers.
4 What your name is?
5 Her husband gos to work in the evening.
6 My sister studys German.
7 Where live you?
8 Where you from?

2 LISTENING

a ▶ **4.6** Listen to the conversation. Put the subjects in the order you hear them.

- [ ] a holiday
- [ ] language lessons
- [ ] working at a university
- [ ] parents
- [1] studying at a university

b ▶ **4.6** Listen again and <u>underline</u> the correct words.

1 *Bob / Kerry* has a job.
2 *Bob / Kerry* lives in London.
3 *Bob / Kerry* studies at university.
4 *Bob / Kerry* works in Hong Kong.
5 *Bob / Kerry* lives in a house.
6 *Bob / Kerry* has language classes.
7 *Bob / Kerry* is on holiday.
8 *Bob's / Kerry's* parents live in France.

c Complete the conversation with your own ideas.

A Hi, _____!
B Hello, _____. How are you?
A I'm fine, thanks. I'm a student at _____ University now.
B Really? What subject do you _____?
A _____. Where do you _____ now?
B I live in _____ and I work _____ an office.
A That's good.
B How _____ your parents?
A They're fine. They live in _____ now.
B Really? That's great.

2 VOCABULARY

Tick (✓) the sentences that are correct. Correct the mistakes.

1 [✓] I teach children.
2 [ ] Our English class has six woman and two men.
3 [ ] I speak Italian.
4 [ ] My sister is twenty and five years old.
5 [ ] I study at high school.
6 [ ] Their son is thirty-three and their daugter is thirty-five.
7 [ ] His mother is hundred years old.
8 [ ] I meet interesting peoples at work.

⟲ REVIEW YOUR PROGRESS

Look again at Review your progress on p.14 of the Student's Book. How well can you do these things now?
3 = very well   2 = well   1 = not so well

I CAN ...

talk about my life and ask about others	[ ]
talk about my family	[ ]
ask and talk about photos.	[ ]

5A There are lots of old houses

1 GRAMMAR
there is / there are: positive

a Put the words in the correct order to make sentences.

1 here / there / 's / school / one .
   <u>There's one school here.</u>
2 teachers / two / there / are .
   _____
3 cars / are / few / a / there .
   _____
4 a / there / 's / small / museum .
   _____
5 are / families / ten / there .
   _____
6 there / old / an / 's / hospital .
   _____

b ▶ 5.1 Listen and check.

c Complete the sentences with *there's* or *there are*.

1 <u>There are</u> lots of people.
2 _____ a good café in the old town.
3 _____ an interesting shop on this street.
4 _____ about 50 families.
5 _____ a few new homes and flats.
6 _____ a very small school.
7 _____ 72 big houses.
8 _____ one bank.

2 PRONUNCIATION
Sound and spelling: /uː/ and /ʌ/

a ▶ 5.2 Listen to the words in the box. What sound do the **marked** letters have? Complete the table.

f**ew**	b**u**tter	s**o**metimes	s**u**permarket	sch**oo**l	st**u**dy
be**au**tiful	p**oo**l	l**o**ve	wh**o**	f**u**nny	m**o**ther

Sound 1 /uː/ (e.g. *you*)	Sound 2 /ʌ/ (e.g. *cup*)
few	

3 VOCABULARY Places in a town

a Write the words under the pictures.

park hospital ~~shop~~ hotel beach café cinema
school bank station restaurant swimming pool

1 _____shop_____

2 _____

3 _____

4 _____

5 _____ 6 _____

7 _____ 8 _____

9 _____ 10 _____

11 _____ 12 _____

1 GRAMMAR there is / there are: negative and questions

a Tick (✓) the correct words to complete the sentences.

1 There isn't _____ in the room.
   a ✓ a TV   b ☐ two TVs

2 Are there any good _____ in this town?
   a ☐ restaurant   b ☐ restaurants

3 There aren't _____ on the first floor.
   a ☐ a big room   b ☐ any big rooms

4 There aren't any _____ here.
   a ☐ car park   b ☐ car parks

5 Is there _____ near here?
   a ☐ a café   b ☐ any cafés

6 Is there _____ near the station?
   a ☐ a bank   b ☐ banks

b Underline the correct words to complete the conversations.

Conversation 1

A ¹There is / Is there a bath in the room?

B No, there ²isn't / aren't. But there ³are / is a shower.

Conversation 2

A There ⁴aren't any / isn't a hotels in this town.

B Oh.

A ⁵There aren't any / There's a hostel on King Street. It's very good.

B OK. Thanks.

Conversation 3

B Is there ⁶any / a car park for this hotel?

A Yes, ⁷there is / is there.

B ⁸Are there any / Is there an empty rooms on the ground floor?

A No, there ⁹aren't / isn't. Sorry. There ¹⁰are / isn't lots of empty rooms on the top floor.

B Oh … No thanks.

c ▶5.3 Listen and check.

2 PRONUNCIATION
Sound and spelling: /ʃ/

a ▶5.4 Listen and tick (✓) the words that have the /ʃ/ sound.

1	bath	☐	7	six	☐
2	shower	☐	8	finish	☐
3	China	☐	9	museum	☐
4	Russia	☐	10	shop	☐
5	she	☐	11	station	☐
6	sure	☐	12	cinema	☐

3 VOCABULARY Hotels

a Complete the sentences. Use the letters in brackets.

1 There's a big _____bath_____ but there isn't any hot water. (a h b t)

2 It's very cold. Can I have a _____ for my bed, please? (n e k l a b t)

3 There's free _____-_____ here, but I don't have my computer with me. (f i i w)

4 The _____'s very good and there's lots of hot water. (o r w s h e)

5 There's a big _____ for meetings on the second floor. (o m o r)

6 Can I have a _____, please? I want to go to the swimming pool. (o w e l t)

7 **A** Where's the car?
   B It's in the _____ _____. (p r a c k r a)

8 There's one small _____ on the bed. (w o l p l i)

b Complete the crossword puzzle.

→ Across

1 I often sit in a _____bath_____ of hot water to relax.

3 There are lots of cars in the car _____.

4 **A** Jason's at the swimming pool.
   B Has he got his _____?
   A Oh no! It's on his bed.

6 **A** Can I have a _____?
   B Sorry, there isn't any hot water.

↓ Down

1 **A** I'm cold.
   B Put a _____ on the bed.

2 Do you like watching films on _____ or at the cinema?

3 **A** There are three big _____ on my bed.
   B Give me one for my head.

5 **A** There isn't any _____-_____.
   B Oh, that's OK – I don't have a phone or a computer with me!

7 We need two _____ at the hotel. One for my parents and one for my brother and me.

5C Everyday English
Is there a supermarket near here?

1 USEFUL LANGUAGE
Asking and saying where things are

a Complete the sentences and questions with the words in the box.

it's	near	~~where's~~	there	there's

1 __Where's__ the hospital?
2 Is _____ a park near here?
3 Are there any restaurants _____ here?
4 _____ one in this street.
5 _____ in the next street.

b Complete the conversation with the sentences in the box.

OK. And is there a museum near here?
Oh yes! Great! Thanks for your help.
~~Excuse me, can you help me?~~
Is there a cinema near here?

A [1]Excuse me, can you help me? _____
B Yes, of course.
A [2]_____
B No, I'm sorry there aren't any cinemas near here. But there are two in the city centre.
A [3]_____
B Yes, there is. It's in this street. Just over there.
A [4]_____
B No problem.

c ▶ 5.5 Listen and check.

d Complete the conversation. Write one word in each gap.
A Excuse me, [1]____can____ you help me?
B Yes, of [2]_____.
A Are there any hotels [3]_____ here?
B Yes, there are. There's one in the [4]_____ street.
A Oh, good. And are there [5]_____ hostels – cheap hostels?
B No, I'm [6]_____, there aren't.
A OK. Thanks [7]_____ your help.
B [8]_____ problem.

e ▶ 5.6 Listen and check.

2 PRONUNCIATION
Emphasising what you say 1

a ▶ 5.7 Listen to the sentences. Which words are stressed? Tick (✓) the correct box.

1 a ☐ It's a very <u>good</u> hotel.
   b ✓ It's a <u>very</u> good hotel.
2 a ☐ It's <u>so</u> hot today!
   b ☐ It's so hot <u>today</u>!
3 a ☐ I'm <u>really</u> sorry.
   b ☐ I'm really <u>sorry</u>.
4 a ☐ This <u>room's</u> really nice.
   b ☐ This room's <u>really</u> nice.
5 a ☐ It's a very big <u>school</u>.
   b ☐ It's a <u>very</u> big school.
6 a ☐ This TV is <u>so</u> old!
   b ☐ This TV is so <u>old</u>!
7 a ☐ The museum's <u>really</u> boring.
   b ☐ The <u>museum's</u> really boring.
8 a ☐ The car park's very <u>small</u>.
   b ☐ The car park's <u>very</u> small.

1 READING

a Read the email. Are the sentences true or false?

1 The hotel is near the station.
2 Marnie and Kalina don't like the hotel.
3 Marnie and Kalina like the things in their room.
4 The hotel is expensive.
5 The hotel has lots of empty rooms.
6 Marnie and Kalina like the hotel manager.
7 There's a restaurant in the hotel.
8 Marnie and Kalina play the guitar in the evening.

2 WRITING SKILLS *and* and *but*

a Tick (✓) the correct ending for the sentences.

1 I live in Rome but …
   a ☐ I speak Italian.
   b ☑ I don't speak Italian.

2 The cinema's big but …
   a ☐ it's very old.
   b ☐ it's great.

3 The high school is good and …
   a ☐ he'd like to study there.
   b ☐ he wouldn't like to study there.

4 The café has great cakes and …
   a ☐ it's got free wi-fi.
   b ☐ it hasn't got free wi-fi.

5 There isn't a bookshop but …
   a ☐ there is a library.
   b ☐ there isn't a library.

6 My office is nice and …
   a ☐ it isn't near my house.
   b ☐ it's near my house.

b Complete the sentences with *and* or *but*.

1 There's a bath ____and____ there's a shower.
2 The room is small _____ it's OK.
3 There's a supermarket in the next street _____ it isn't very big.
4 The city is beautiful _____ it's boring.
5 The hotel has big rooms _____ they're very beautiful.
6 There's a café on the ground floor _____ there's a TV room on the first floor.
7 It's a lovely hotel _____ they don't have any empty rooms.
8 There's a shower _____ there isn't any hot water!

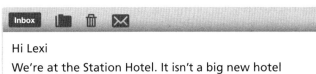

Hi Lexi

We're at the Station Hotel. It isn't a big new hotel near the station – it's an old station near the beach! It's great! The rooms are small but they're very good.

Our room is on the first floor. We have beautiful flowers in the room and there are lots of pillows and blankets on the beds. It isn't cheap but we're only here for three nights.

There are lots of people here. There aren't any empty rooms! All the people are very friendly and the manager's nice. In the evenings we have dinner in the Old Station restaurant. It's in the hotel. The food is good and an old man plays the guitar.

See you soon,

Marnie and Kalina

3 WRITING

a Imagine that you are in a hotel in a new town. Write an email to a friend. Describe the hotel and the town.

Hi

See you soon,

UNIT 5
Reading and listening extension

1 READING

a Read the texts. Tick (✓) the places you read about.

1 a bank ☐
2 a swimming pool ☐
3 a cinema ☐
4 a hospital ☐
5 a hotel ☐
6 a car park ☐
7 a museum ☐
8 a park ☐
9 a school ✓
10 a supermarket ☐

b Read the texts again. <u>Underline</u> the correct words to complete the sentences.

1 *Daria / <u>Gerry</u> / Ellen* lives near a supermarket.
2 *Daria / Gerry / Ellen* doesn't have any children.
3 The hospital is on *Holly Road / High Street / Station Road*.
4 *Holly Road / High Street / Station Road* is a good place to see films.
5 The park is near *Holly Road / High Street / Station Road*.
6 There's a *station / museum / park* on High Street.
7 Daria takes her son to the *swimming pool / ice cream shop / cinema* in summer.
8 There are lots of *shops / cafés / offices* near Gerry's home.

c Write about your street. Think about these questions:

- What is the name of your street?
- Where is your street?
- What is there in or near your street?
- Is it an interesting place to live or work?

MY STREET

I work in the town centre but I live in Station Road. Station Road isn't near the town centre but it is a nice place. There are about 60 houses and there's a school, and a shop where I buy bread every day. There's also a little park near the station. It has an ice cream shop and in summer I sometimes take my son to the park and we have ice cream.

1 DARIA

I live on Holly Road with my wife and daughter. It's not a very interesting place to live but it's easy to get to work because I work at Holly Road Hospital. There are lots of offices and flats in my road but there aren't any shops or restaurants. It isn't a problem – there's a big supermarket near Holly Road and there are lots of buses to the town centre.

2 GERRY

I live and work on High Street, in the centre of the town. There are lots of different shops and cafés here and two bookshops. I work in the bookshop near the museum. When I'm not at work, I sometimes go to the cinema. High Street is a good place to live. My flat is on the first floor and I sometimes sit and watch the people in the street. There is always something interesting to see.

3 ELLEN

Tourist Information Centre

2 LISTENING

a ▶ **5.8** Listen to Mike and a receptionist at a tourist office. Are the sentences true or false?

1 It is summer.
2 There are lots of empty rooms.
3 Mike has a lot of money.
4 Mike chooses a room at the Star Hostel.

b ▶ **5.8** Listen again. Complete the table with the words in the box.

café   cheap   friendly   expensive   free wi-fi
~~near the beach~~   small clean rooms   rooms with baths
TVs in rooms   free breakfast   near the station
rooms with showers

Hotel Splendour	Star Hostel
near the beach	

c ▶ **5.8** Listen again. Underline the correct words.

1 Mike wants a room for a *weekend* /*week*.
2 The room is for *one person* / *two people*.
3 He wants to stay near the *station* / *beach*.
4 Rooms at the Hotel Splendour are *$140* / *$160*.
5 Single rooms at the Star Hostel are *$40* / *$60*.
6 There is a café on the *ground* / *first* floor of the Star Hostel.
7 There are *two* / *three* supermarkets near the hostel.
8 *Mike* / *The receptionist* phones the hostel.

d Complete the conversation with your own ideas.

RECEPTIONIST	Good morning. Can I help?
VISITOR	Hi. I'd like a hotel room for _____ nights near the _____.
RECEPTIONIST	The Royal Hotel is near there. The rooms have _____ and _____, and it's _____ dollars a night.
VISITOR	That's very expensive. I don't have a lot of money.
RECEPTIONIST	Well, there's the Comfort Hotel in this street. They don't have _____ but they're cheap.
VISITOR	OK.
RECEPTIONIST	Do you want me to phone them?
VISITOR	Yes, please.

 **Review**

1 GRAMMAR

Tick (✓) the sentences that are correct. Correct the mistakes.

1 ☐ There is a park here?
     Is there a park here?
2 ☐ There is two cinemas.
3 ☐ There aren't any supermarkets.
4 ☐ Are there any cafés in this street?
5 ☐ No, there not.
6 ☐ Is there a hotel near here?
7 ☐ Yes, there's.
8 ☐ There not any shops here.

2 VOCABULARY

Correct the spelling.

1 I like this restarant.
   I like this restaurant.
2 Where's the scool?
3 Is there a swiming pool?
4 Can I have a blankit, please?
5 There isn't a pilow on the bed.
6 Where's the hospittal?
7 We often go to the beech.
8 Do you have a towl?

⟳ REVIEW YOUR PROGRESS

Look again at Review your progress on p.46 of the Student's Book. How well can you do these things now?
3 = very well   2 = well   1 = not so well

I CAN ...

describe a town	☐
talk about hotels and hostels	☐
ask about and say where places are.	☐

1 GRAMMAR
Present simple: *he / she / it* negative

a Underline the correct words.

1 Shona *don't* / *doesn't* work in an office.
2 I *don't* / *doesn't* work on Wednesdays.
3 Tom doesn't *meet* / *meets* interesting people in his job.
4 We *don't* / *doesn't* speak a lot at work.
5 Mark *don't* / *doesn't* study Italian. He studies Spanish.
6 Sheila doesn't *likes* / *like* her job.
7 You *don't* / *doesn't* live here!
8 He *don't* / *doesn't* eat meat.

b Complete the sentences with the correct form of the verbs in brackets.

1 Megan __doesn't eat__ cake, biscuits or ice cream. (not / eat)
2 You _____ young children. (not / teach)
3 Anton _____ coffee. (not / like)
4 My brother _____ in this house. (not / live)
5 My parents _____. (not / work)
6 Debbie _____ to the cinema with her friends. (not / go)
7 I _____ his name. (not / know)
8 The doctor _____ Spanish. (not / speak)

2 VOCABULARY Jobs

a Write the words under the pictures.

chef   doctor   factory worker   football player
office worker   receptionist   shop assistant
student   ~~taxi driver~~   waiter

b Underline the correct words.

1 Hello, I'm Natasha. I'm the hotel *assistant* / *receptionist*.
2 **A** What's your brother's job?
  B He's a *businessman* / *businesswoman*.
3 I'm an IT *worker* / *player*. I work with computers.
4 I'm a taxi *worker* / *driver*. I sometimes work at night.
5 I work in this restaurant. I'm a *teacher* / *chef*.
6 Lionel Messi is a football *assistant* / *player*.
7 **A** What's your sister's job?
  B She's a *waiter* / *waitress*.
8 **A** Excuse me! Are you a shop *assistant* / *driver*?
  B Yes, I am. Can I help you?

c ▶ 6.1 Listen and check.

3 PRONUNCIATION
Sound and spelling: /ɜː/

a ▶ 6.2 Listen and tick (✓) the words that have the /ɜː/ sound.

1 park	☐	7 thirty	☐
2 here	☐	8 thirteen	☐
3 girl	☐	9 fruit	☐
4 world	☐	10 Turkey	☐
5 sport	☐	11 wrong	☐
6 work	☐	12 university	☐

1 __taxi driver__

2 _____

3 _____

4 _____

5 _____

6 _____

7 _____

8 _____

9 _____

10 _____

6B I wake up at 4:00

1 GRAMMAR
Present simple: *he / she / it* questions

a Put the words in the correct order to make questions.

1 your / up / husband / early / get / does ?
   Does your husband get up early?

2 Eduardo / work / does / where ?
   _____

3 up / does / what / Richard / wake / time ?
   _____

4 does / evening / get / how / Amy / in / the / home ?
   _____

5 have / home / at / does / breakfast / Carol ?
   _____

6 what / work / do / your / sister / does / at ?
   _____

b Complete the sentences with the words in the box.

> do Kathy   does she   does your husband
> he does   ~~does Lottie live~~   Martin get

1 **A** Where _does Lottie live_ ?
   B In Germany.
2 **A** _____ work at night?
   B No, he doesn't.
3 When does _____ home?
4 What time _____ wake up in the morning?
5 When _____ and Jim finish work?
6 **A** Does he study English?
   B Yes, _____.

c ▶6.3 Listen and check.

2 VOCABULARY Daily routine

a Put the daily routine in the correct order.

- [ ] finish work
- [ ] get up
- [ ] go to bed
- [ ] go to work
- [ ] have dinner
- [ ] have lunch
- [ ] start work
- [1] wake up

b Complete the sentences with the verbs in the box.

> arrive   finish   get   go (x2)   have   start   ~~wake~~

1 I ____wake____ up at 7:00 am and I _____ up at 7:15 am.
2 I _____ breakfast at home.
3 I _____ to work every day.
4 I _____ work at 9:00 am and I _____ work at 5:30 pm.
5 I _____ home at 6:30 pm.
6 I _____ to bed at 11:00 pm.

c ▶6.4 Listen and check.

3 PRONUNCIATION Consonant groups

a ▶6.5 Listen and complete the words. Write two letters to make a consonant group.

1 t w enty
2 _ _ eakfast
3 _ _ anish

4 _ _ ay
5 _ _ uit
6 _ _ ass

6C Everyday English
I'll come with you

1 USEFUL LANGUAGE
Making and accepting offers

a Underline the correct words to complete the conversation.

DAN [1]*Do / Would* you like a cup of tea?
EVA Yes, please.
DAN And [2]*you would / would you* like a piece of cake?
EVA No, [3]*OK / it's OK*, thanks.
DAN I need to go to the shops for bread.
EVA I'll [4]*can come / come* with you.
DAN [5]*That / That's* great, thanks. And I need to make some sandwiches.
EVA [6]*I / I'll* help you.
DAN Thank you, [7]*it's / that's* very kind.

b ▶ 6.6 Listen and check.

c Put the conversation in the correct order.

☐ **MEG** I need to make lunch for Jake and Carrie.
☐ **MEG** And would you like a piece of cake?
☐ **MEG** All right. Thanks. We need pizzas.
☐ **MEG** Don't worry. It's OK. The pizzas at the supermarket are fine.
☐ **MEG** Thank you. That's great.
1 **MEG** Would you like a cup of coffee, Rob?
☐ **ROB** No, I'm fine, thanks – just coffee, please.
☐ **ROB** I'll help you.
☐ **ROB** I can make pizzas. I make very good pizzas!
☐ **ROB** Yes, please.
☐ **ROB** OK, I'll go to the supermarket.

d ▶ 6.7 Listen and check.

2 PRONUNCIATION
Emphasising what you say 2

a ▶ 6.8 Listen to the sentences. Which words are stressed? Tick (✓) the correct box.

1 **A** I need to make dinner for eight people!
   B a ☐ I <u>can</u> help you.
      b ✓ <u>I</u> can help you.

2 **A** I need to go to the supermarket but I'm really busy.
   B a ☐ I'll <u>go</u>.
      b ☐ <u>I'll</u> go.

3 **A** Oh no! I haven't got any money with me!
   B a ☐ <u>I</u> can pay.
      b ☐ I can <u>pay</u>.

4 **A** I can't open this bottle of water!
   B a ☐ <u>I'll</u> do it.
      b ☐ I'll <u>do</u> it.

5 **A** I need to go to the shops. Can you drive me?
   B a ☐ Sorry, but I'm really busy. Jim can take <u>you</u>.
      b ☐ Sorry, but I'm really busy. <u>Jim</u> can take you.

6 **A** I need some cups. Do you have any cups?
   B a ☐ No, I don't. <u>I</u> can give you some glasses.
      b ☐ No, I don't. I can give you some <u>glasses</u>.

1 READING

a Read the email and tick (✓) the correct answers.

| Inbox | | | |

Hi Mum

Life here in New York is exciting!

I have a job in a café in Manhattan. I get up at half past four in the morning every day from Monday to Saturday and I work from half past five until two o'clock in the afternoon.

There are lots of people in the café from six until nine o'clock because the breakfasts here are great! I really like the breakfasts! The sandwiches are also very good and I have lunch there every day.

I have a new friend in New York. His name's Rex and he's a taxi driver. He often works at night and he has breakfast in the café at half past five. He always says 'Coffee and breakfast for dinner, please!' Then he goes home and he goes to bed!

Email me soon!

Love,

Ivan

1 Where does Ivan work?
  a ☐ in a restaurant
  b ☐ in a shop
  c ✓ in a café

2 What time does Ivan get up?
  a ☐ 4:30 am
  b ☐ 5:30 am
  c ☐ 6:30 am

3 Ivan doesn't work on _____.
  a ☐ Mondays
  b ☐ Saturdays
  c ☐ Sundays

4 What time does Ivan start work?
  a ☐ 5:30 am
  b ☐ 9:00 am
  c ☐ 2:00 pm

5 Ivan likes _____ at the café.
  a ☐ the breakfasts
  b ☐ the sandwiches
  c ☐ the breakfasts and the sandwiches

6 Rex goes to the café at 5:30 am because he
_____.
  a ☐ always starts work at 6:00 am
  b ☐ often finishes work in the morning
  c ☐ works at the café

2 WRITING SKILLS *because* and *also*

a Correct the mistakes.

1 Diana's a taxi driver. Because she likes driving.
  Diana's a taxi driver because she likes driving.

2 They have breakfast at school. They have also lunch at school.
  _____

3 I study at university. I also am a waitress.
  _____

4 She gets up early. She goes also to bed early.
  _____

5 He's a teacher because he gets up early.
  _____

6 She sometimes works at night. Because she's a doctor.
  _____

b Complete the sentences with *also* or *because*.

1 There's a museum in my home town. There's ____*also*____ a cinema.
2 She speaks Japanese _____ her mum's from Japan.
3 I play football. I _____ play tennis.
4 He goes to bed at 8 am _____ he works at night.
5 My parents have got a cat _____ they love animals.
6 I've got black hair. My brother's _____ got black hair.

3 WRITING

a Write an email about the daily routine of one of your friends or a member of your family. Use the email in 1 to help you.

| ← | ✉ | ▲ ▼ |

UNIT 6
Reading and listening extension

1 READING

a Read the magazine article. Complete the sentences with the words in the box.

---
at night   in the afternoon   in the evening
in the morning   at the weekend
---

1 Steffi sees her friends _____.
2 She has classes at the university _____.
3 She goes to the university library _____.
4 From Monday to Friday, she goes to work _____.
5 She works until 11:30 _____.

b Read the article again. Are the sentences true or false?

1 Steffi studies in her home country.
2 Steffi likes her course.
3 Her classes start at 8 am.
4 She doesn't go home in the afternoon.
5 She has dinner at home.
6 She goes to work after dinner.
7 She finishes work at 11:30.
8 She works all weekend.

c Write a short description of your day. Think about these questions:

• What time do you get up and go to bed?
• What do you do in the morning, afternoon and evening?
• When do you see your friends?

University *life*

University is expensive in the USA and students also need to pay for course books, food and a place to live. A lot of students work to get extra money. Is it a good idea? We ask a student.

Steffi, 23

I'm a student in New York, but I'm from Hamburg in Germany. I love my course but New York is expensive so I work in a cinema in the evenings and on Saturdays.

My day usually starts at 7:45 am when I get up and have breakfast. Then I go to my classes at the university. They start at 9:00 am and finish at 12:30 pm. There aren't any classes in the afternoon so I study in the university library. I have something to eat in the student restaurant and I walk to the cinema. My working hours are 6:00 pm to 11:30 pm from Monday to Friday, and 1:30 pm to 11:30 pm on Saturdays. Sunday is my free day and I play tennis or go to a museum with my friends.

My job is OK but I don't want to work six days a week. I get home late and I only have six or seven hours' sleep. Sometimes, I feel very tired in my classes and I want to sleep, which isn't good.

2 LISTENING

a ⊙ **6.9** Listen to the interview. Underline the correct answers.

1 Ian Baker is *Scottish* / *English*.
2 He is a *factory worker* / *businessman*.
3 Ian is *single* / *married*.
4 Ian and Rita have a factory in *Aberdeen* / *Glasgow*.
5 *Eighty* / *Ninety* people work in the factory.
6 Their customers are in *Europe* / *Asia* and South America.

b ⊙ **6.9** Listen again and underline the correct words.

1 Ian and Rita *have* / *don't have* a computer shop in Scotland.
2 The factory *makes* / *doesn't make* computers for hospitals.
3 Ian *works* / *doesn't work* about 12 hours a day.
4 Ian *sits* / *doesn't sit* in his office every day.
5 Ian *meets* / *doesn't meet* the people who use his computers.
6 Ian and Rita *have* / *don't have* customers in the UK.
7 Ian *speaks* / *doesn't speak* a foreign language.
8 Rita *goes* / *doesn't go* to South America with Ian.

c Complete the conversation with your own ideas.

INTERVIEWER	Welcome to the show. This week we're talking to people who live and work in _____. Today, my guest is _____. Where in _____ do you live?
GUEST	I live in _____.
INTERVIEWER	And what do you do?
GUEST	I'm a _____.
INTERVIEWER	That's interesting. Do you like your work?
GUEST	_____ because _____.
INTERVIEWER	Do you work long hours?
GUEST	_____.
INTERVIEWER	And do you visit places for work?
GUEST	_____.
INTERVIEWER	Thanks very much for talking to us today.

⊙ Review

1 GRAMMAR

Correct the mistakes.

1 Lee doesn't works on Mondays.
  Lee doesn't work on Mondays.
2 Does he speaks English?
3 When Anna arrives home?
4 Pedro like fish?
5 Seb not plays tennis.
6 **A** Does Becky live here?
  B Yes, she lives.
7 **A** Does Russell have a computer?
  B No, he not.
8 Where she lives?

2 VOCABULARY

Tick (✓) the sentences that are correct. Correct the mistakes.

1 ✓ I wake up at 6:30 am.
2 ☐ He gets up at 6:30 am.
3 ☐ She's a driver taxi.
4 ☐ I have a lunch at work.
5 ☐ He's a businesman.
6 ☐ She's a chef.
7 ☐ I'm a receptionist.
8 ☐ I go bed at 11:00 pm.

⟳ REVIEW YOUR PROGRESS

Look again at Review your progress on p.54 of the Student's Book. How well can you do these things now?
3 = very well   2 = well   1 = not so well

I CAN ...

talk about people's jobs	☐
talk about daily routines and habits	☐
make and accept offers.	☐

7A How much are these books?

1 GRAMMAR this, that, these, those

a Complete the sentences with the words in the box.

> this   that   these   those

1 Do you like _____ flowers?
2 Do you like _____ flowers?
3 I'd like _____ car.
4 I want _____ car!

b ▶ 7.1 Listen and check.

c Complete the sentences with *this*, *that*, *these* or *those*. Remember *near* = here (near me) and *far* = there (not near me).

1 ___That___ picture's interesting. (far)
2 _____ plates are nice. (near)
3 I like _____ chair. (near)
4 How much is _____ guitar? (far)
5 I like _____ shop. (near)
6 _____ bags are beautiful. (far)
7 I don't like _____ lamp. (far)
8 How much are _____ books? (near)

2 VOCABULARY Common objects 2

a Complete the sentences with the words in the box.

> book   cup   ~~clock~~   football   guitar
> picture   plant   plate   radio   suitcase

1 What time is it? There isn't a ___clock___ in this room.
2 Can I have a _____ for this pizza, please?
3 Would you like to have a _____ of tea?
4 I have lots of clothes, but this bag's very small. I need a big _____.
5 I have a great _____ of my family. Do you want to see it?
6 This is my English _____. It's called *Empower*.
7 Simon teaches young children. He often takes his _____ to school for music lessons.
8 I like to listen to the _____ in the evening. They talk about interesting things.
9 What's that _____ in the garden? The flowers are very nice.
10 Look, it's an old _____! Would you like to play a game?

3 VOCABULARY Prices

a Tick (✓) the correct words.

1 This glass is €10.50.
   a ☐ ten euros and fifty
   b ✓ ten euros fifty
   c ☐ one hundred and five euros

2 This football is £30.
   a ☐ thirty pound
   b ☐ thirteen pounds
   c ☐ thirty pounds

3 That guitar is $129.99.
   a ☐ one hundred and ninety-nine dollars
   b ☐ one hundred and twenty-nine dollars ninety-nine
   c ☐ one hundred and nine-twenty dollars nine-ninety

4 That radio is €24.75.
   a ☐ twenty-four euros seventy-five
   b ☐ forty-two euros seventy-five
   c ☐ seventy-five euros twenty-four

5 Those cups are £9.50.
   a ☐ ninety-five pounds
   b ☐ nine pounds fifty
   c ☐ five pounds ninety

6 These plants are $3.89.
   a ☐ three dollars eighty-nine
   b ☐ three dollar eighty-nine
   c ☐ three of dollars eighty-nine

b ▶ 7.2 Listen and check.

4 PRONUNCIATION
Sound and spelling: /b/, /p/, /g/ and /

a ▶ 7.3 Listen to the words. Write the missing letters.

1 _football
2 suit_ase
3 _lass
4 _a_
5 _late
6 lam_
7 _uitar
8 _oo_
9 _up
10 _lant

7B It's Greg's T-shirt

1 GRAMMAR
Possessive 's; Revision of adverbs

a Put the words in the correct order to make sentences. Add an apostrophe (') where possible. There may be more than one possible answer.

1 bag / it's / Kates .
   It's Kate's bag.
2 Darrens / they're / shoes .
   _____
3 brown / friends / jacket's / my .
   _____
4 the / are / new / boys / trousers .
   _____
5 I / jeans / never / wear .
   _____
6 clothes / I / my / sisters / sometimes / wear .
   _____

b ⏵ **7.4** Listen and check.

c Complete the sentences with the names in brackets and the possessive 's.

1 This is _____Emma's_____ T-shirt. (Emma)
2 Where's _____ phone? (Mehmet)
3 I like _____ new house. (Andrew and Mina)
4 That's _____ computer. (the girls)
5 What's _____ phone number? (Sally)
6 I like _____ shoes. (the children)

2 VOCABULARY Clothes and colours

a Complete the sentences with the words in the box.

| black | blue | brown | green | ~~grey~~ | red | white | yellow |

1 Older people often have _____grey_____ hair.
2 Chocolate is usually _____.
3 Bananas are _____.
4 Milk is _____.
5 Strawberries are _____.
6 Grass is _____.
7 A tiger is orange and _____.
8 On a sunny day, the sky is _____.

b Complete the crossword puzzle.

→ Across
2 The opposite of 'dark'.
5 _____ + white = pink.
6 It's difficult to walk in these _____! They're very big!
9 These are usually blue. You wear them on your legs. They come from the USA.

↓ Down
1 I wear _____glasses_____ to read a book or use the computer.
3 You wear _____ on your legs.
4 Eggs are white and _____.
7 Men wear this to work. They wear it on their body.
8 Old photos are _____ and white.

3 PRONUNCIATION
Sound and spelling: /ʃ/ and /dʒ/

a ⏵ **7.5** Listen to the words in the box. What sound do the **marked** letters have? Complete the table.

| ~~jeans~~ large fashion shoes nationality Japanese vegetables shirt Germany sure village shop |

Sound 1 /ʃ/ (e.g. *she*)	Sound 2 /dʒ/ (e.g. *change*)
	jeans

41

1 USEFUL LANGUAGE Going shopping

a Complete the conversations with the sentences in the box.

> Here's your receipt.
> Can I look around?
> ~~Enter your PIN, please.~~
> I'd like that T-shirt, please.
> How much are these bags?

1 **A** That's £52.95, please.
  B Can I use a card to pay?
  A Yes. <u>Enter your PIN, please.</u>
2 **A** Can I help you?
  B _____
  A Of course.
3 **A** _____
  B Thanks.
4 **A** _____
  B They're £35 each.
5 **A** _____
  B Certainly. Here you are.

b ▶️**7.6** Listen and check.

c Put the conversation in the correct order.

☐	**SHOP ASSISTANT**	Thank you.
1	**SHOP ASSISTANT**	Can I help you?
☐	**SHOP ASSISTANT**	Certainly. That's £16, please.
☐	**SHOP ASSISTANT**	They're £4 each.
☐	**SHOP ASSISTANT**	OK, here you are.
☐	**SHOP ASSISTANT**	Of course. Enter your PIN, please. OK, here's your receipt. Would you like a bag?
☐	**CUSTOMER**	OK, I'd like four white plates, please.
☐	**CUSTOMER**	Can I use a card to pay?
☐	**CUSTOMER**	Thank you very much.
☐	**CUSTOMER**	No, don't worry.
☐	**CUSTOMER**	Yes, how much are these white plates?

d ▶️**7.7** Listen and check.

2 PRONUNCIATION Joining words

a ▶️**7.8** Listen to the sentences. What are the extra sounds? Tick (✓) the correct box.

	/j/	/w/
1 Here you‿are.		✓
2 Is it blue‿or green?		
3 Three‿apples, please.		
4 Are you‿OK?		
5 She‿only wears white.		
6 These cups are for me‿and you.		
7 He‿always wears black.		
8 There are two‿empty bags.		

1 READING

a Read emails 1–6. Which advertisement A–D is each email about? Tick (✓) the correct box.

Ⓐ **FOR SALE**
Old books, photos, magazines and newspapers. Very interesting! Good prices.

Ⓑ **FOR SALE**
Beautiful 1960s plates, cups, bowls and glasses! Not expensive!

Ⓒ **FOR SALE**
Bed, tables and chairs. I also have some great lamps and pictures for sale.

Ⓓ **FOR SALE**
New! Men's trousers, shirts, jackets and coats. Very good condition! I also have shoes, umbrellas and watches for sale.

		A	B	C	D
1	You have an online ad for men's clothes. Do you also sell women's clothes?				✓
2	I saw your online advertisement for a bed. I'd like to buy it!				
3	I saw your advertisement. You have some interesting things for sale. How much is the watch? Is it old or new?'				
4	I saw your advertisement for things you want to sell. I'd like to see a photo of the bowls, please.				
5	I have a few questions about the things in your ad. Are the photos colour or black and white? Do you have any DVDs? How old are the newspapers?				
6	I saw your advertisement and I need four chairs for my flat. How many do you have? How old are they?				

2 WRITING SKILLS
Commas, exclamation marks and question marks

a Tick (✓) the correct ending for the sentences.

1 How much is the …
   a ☐ plant   b ☐ plant!   c ✓ plant?

2 Good …
   a ☐ prices,   b ☐ prices!   c ☐ prices?

3 Hats for sale: we have …
   a ☐ red white green blue and yellow
   b ☐ red, white, green, blue, and yellow,
   c ☐ red, white, green, blue and yellow.

4 Can I pay …
   a ☐ online,   b ☐ online!   c ☐ online?

5 Beautiful …
   a ☐ bags, and shoes.
   b ☐ bags and shoes.
   c ☐ bags! and shoes!

6 I'd like to buy …
   a ☐ a picture, a bowl, a lamp and a book.
   b ☐ a picture, a bowl, a lamp and a book?
   c ☐ a picture, a bowl a lamp and a book

7 How old is …
   a ☐ it,   b ☐ it!   c ☐ it?

8 We need some …
   a ☐ cups, plates and glasses.
   b ☐ cups plates and glasses
   c ☐ cups, plates, and glasses?

b Add a comma (,), an exclamation mark (!) or a question mark (?) to each sentence.

1 How old are you
   <u>How old are you?</u>

2 You're a grandmother
   _____

3 I've got a sandwich a drink and a banana.
   _____

4 These shoes are very expensive
   _____

5 Where is the station
   _____

6 Satako Kai and Berto are in my class.
   _____

3 WRITING

a Write an email. Reply to this advert. You have a new house and you need furniture and two computers.

FURNITURE FOR SALE!
We have chairs, tables, clocks and technology items for sale. Good condition! Contact Jason.   **Reply to this advert**

> Hi
>
>
>
>
>
>
> Thanks

---

1 READING

a Read the article and match a–d to paragraphs 1–4.

a ☐ What I wear when I'm not at work
b ☐ Where I buy my clothes
c ☐ What I wear for special occasions
d ☐ My work clothes

b Read the article again. Are the sentences true or false?

1 Pete's uniform is blue.
2 The police officers' yellow jackets are useful.
3 Pete's friends like fashionable clothes.
4 His favourite colour is brown.
5 He has an expensive suit for special events.
6 He usually wears a dark grey shirt for special events.
7 Marks and Spencer is in the shopping mall.
8 Jane's favourite shop is the same as Pete's.

c Choose someone you know. Write a description of their clothes. Think about these questions:

- What clothes do they wear at different times of the day and different days of the week?
- What are their favourite colours?
- Where do they buy their clothes?

MY CLOTHES by Pete Hobbs

1 I don't have to worry about my work clothes. I'm a police officer and I have a uniform. I like the uniform. We wear a dark blue jacket, dark blue trousers and a white shirt. We also have big yellow police jackets to wear when we're outside in the street. These jackets are very useful because people can see that we are police officers.

2 I'm not very interested in fashion. My wife, Jane, says that my clothes are boring but most of my friends' clothes are the same as mine! When I'm not at work I like to wear comfortable clothes, for example jeans and a T-shirt or a jumper. I don't really have a favourite colour, but I try not to wear dark blue because it's the colour of my uniform. My favourite item of clothing is my old brown jacket.

3 I don't have many expensive clothes, but sometimes I go to special events, for example, when friends get married, and I need to wear something nice. I have a suit by the designer Tom Ford. It has dark grey trousers and a matching jacket. I usually wear this with a white shirt and tie.

4 I usually go shopping with Jane. We both like to go to the shopping mall in the centre of town. It has lots of shops and it's easy to find things. My favourite shop there is Marks and Spencer. Marks and Spencer's clothes are usually comfortable and they aren't very expensive. I buy all my clothes there but Jane's favourite shops are Next and Debenhams.

Review

2 LISTENING

a ▶**7.9** Listen to the conversation. What does the shop sell? <u>Underline</u> the correct answer.

books	handbags	computers	birthday cards
things for the home	clothes	chocolates	

b ▶**7.9** Listen again. Tick (✓) the things the people talk about.

1 a birthday   ✓
2 a holiday   ☐
3 a party   ☐
4 a parent   ☐
5 a present   ☐
6 a friend   ☐
7 a new flat   ☐
8 a new car   ☐
9 a birthday card   ☐
10 a postcard   ☐

c ▶**7.9** Listen again and <u>underline</u> the correct words.

1 Paul thinks shopping is *tiring* / *boring*.
2 Sue wants to buy something *useful* / *colourful*.
3 The cups have pictures of *flowers* / *animals* on them.
4 The lamp is *blue* / *brown*.
5 Paul doesn't like the *colour* / *price* of the lamp.
6 Paul's mum wants a table for her *TV* / *laptop*.
7 The table is *£50* / *£60*.
8 Next, Paul and Sue will go to a *café* / *card shop*.

d Write about a shop you like. Think about these questions:

- What's the shop's name?
- Where is it?
- What things do you buy there?
- How often do you go there?
- How many people work there?
- Why do you like it?

1 GRAMMAR

Tick (✓) the sentences that are correct. Correct the mistakes. Remember *near* = here (near me) and *far* = there (not near me).

1 ✓ How much is this chair? (near)
2 ☐ This cups are £6. (near)
3 ☐ That bag is nice. (far)
4 ☐ Those picture is interesting. (far)
5 ☐ I like Martins shoes.
6 ☐ I have two boys. This is the boys' bedroom.
7 ☐ I have one daughter. This is my daughter's hat.
8 ☐ It's Anna's and David's computer.

2 VOCABULARY

Correct the mistakes.

1 I'd like a yellow suitcais.
   I'd like a yellow suitcase.
2 He has a red giutar.
3 This picture is one hundred and sixty-three pound.
4 Do you have any black radioes?
5 It's a light brawn skirt.
6 Where's your green jaket?
7 I have six wite shirts.
8 It's a grey dark coat.

🏁 REVIEW YOUR PROGRESS

Look again at Review your progress on p.62 of the Student's Book. How well can you do these things now?
3 = very well   2 = well   1 = not so well

I CAN ...

talk about things I want to buy	☐
talk about the clothes that people wear	☐
ask about and pay for things in a shop.	☐

8A I was on tour with my band

1 GRAMMAR Past simple: *be*

a Put the words in the correct order to make sentences and questions.

1 last / concert / at / night / was / I / a .
   I was at a concert last night.
2 where / morning / this / Nina / was ?
   _____
3 weren't / last / we / at / night / concert / the .
   _____
4 they / ago / in / week / were / a / Shanghai .
   _____
5 week / were / Moscow / you / in / last ?
   _____
6 were / yes, / we .
   _____
7 the / afternoon / at / meeting / was / this / Adrian ?
   _____
8 no, / wasn't / he .
   _____

b Complete the conversation with *was, were, weren't* or *wasn't*.

A You ¹___weren't___ here on Friday afternoon. Where ²_____ you?
B I ³_____ with my brothers. We ⁴_____ at a basketball game.
A Oh, ⁵_____ it good?
B No, it ⁶_____. I don't like basketball.
A Oh. And where ⁷_____ you on Friday evening?
B We ⁸_____ at a party.
A ⁹_____ it a good party?
B It ¹⁰_____ OK. The people ¹¹_____ really nice, but the music ¹²_____ very good.

c ▶ 8.1 Listen and check.

2 VOCABULARY Past time expressions

a Complete the sentences with the words in the box.

a year ago   last month   last night
this afternoon   this morning   yesterday

2015
3
January

2016
3
January

1 It's January 2016. It was January 2015
   ___a year ago___ .
2 Today it's Sunday the third of January.
   It was the second of January _____.
3 It's Sunday evening. I was at work from 2:00 pm until 5:30 pm today. I was at work _____.
4 It's Sunday evening. I was at work from 8:30 am until 11:30 am today. I was at work _____.
5 It's Sunday. I was at work from 8:00 pm until 11:30 pm on Saturday. I was at work _____.
6 It's January 2016. I was in Rome in December 2015. I was in Rome _____.

b ▶ 8.2 Listen and check.

c Underline the correct words.

1 I was in Paris *at* / *on* / *ago* Thursday.
2 **A** Were you in Bristol *yesterday* / *this yesterday* / *on yesterday*?
   B Yes, I was.
3 Was Adam at work *on* / *this* / *last* morning?
4 They weren't at home *last* / *ago* / *at* the weekend.
5 We were at a concert *the last night* / *on last night* / *last night*.
6 Where were you *three months ago* / *ago three months* / *last three months*?

3 PRONUNCIATION
Sentence stress: *was* and *were* in positive sentences

a ▶ 8.3 Listen and underline the two stressed words in each sentence.

1 James was at home.
2 We were in London.
3 You were at work.
4 My parents were in Italy.
5 The party was fun.
6 The game was exciting.
7 The concert was good.
8 The meetings were interesting.

8B Who killed Lady Grey?

1 GRAMMAR Past simple: positive

a Complete the crossword puzzle with the past simple form of the verbs.

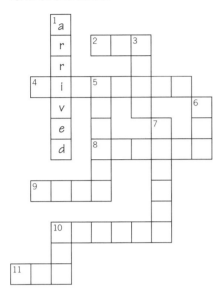

→ Across	↓ Down
2 see	1 arrive
4 listen	3 go
8 kill	5 talk
9 read	6 have
10 stay	7 play
11 get	10 sit

b Complete the story with the past simple form of the verbs in brackets.

A great evening

My friend Max and I ¹___arrived___ (arrive) at the cinema at 5:30 pm and we ²_____ (watch) a film. In the film, a woman ³_____ (be) at a party and she ⁴_____ (kill) a man. It was very exciting!

Then we ⁵_____ (go) to the new café on King Street. I ⁶_____ (see) a man I know from work, Oskar. We asked him to eat with us and he ⁷_____ (say) yes. We ⁸_____ (talk) about the film. Oskar ⁹_____ (know) it too. Max went home at about 8:30 pm but Oskar and I ¹⁰_____ (stay) at the café and ¹¹_____ (have) a coffee.

After, we went to my house and ¹²_____ (play) cards. Oskar was really good! It was a great evening.

2 VOCABULARY Free time activities

a Complete the activities with the words in the box.

go (x2)   have (x2)   listen to   play (x2)   read   watch

1 ___play___ the guitar   2 _____ the radio   3 _____ a shower

4 _____ to the cinema   5 _____ a drink   6 _____ a magazine

7 _____ a computer game   8 _____ a football match   9 _____ shopping

b Underline the correct words.

1 I *listen to* / *read* / *watch* the newspaper every day.
2 I sometimes *go* / *listen to* / *watch* films on TV.
3 I never *go* / *have* / *watch* to the cinema.
4 I don't *listen to* / *play* / *read* magazines.
5 I *go* / *have* / *play* a shower every evening.
6 I usually *listen to* / *read* / *watch* the radio in the morning.
7 I often *read* / *play* / *watch* football matches on TV.
8 I *have* / *play* / *watch* computer games every day.
9 I always *have* / *listen to* / *watch* music in the evening.
10 I always *go* / *play* / *watch* to parties at the weekend.

c ▶8.4 Listen and check.

3 PRONUNCIATION
Sound and spelling: /t/ and /d/

a ▶8.5 Listen to the past simple verbs. Is the final sound /t/ or /d/? Tick (✓) the correct box.

	/t/	/d/
1 talked	✓	☐
2 killed	☐	☐
3 stayed	☐	☐
4 listened	☐	☐
5 played	☐	☐
6 watched	☐	☐
7 helped	☐	☐
8 arrived	☐	☐

8C Everyday English
Let's go somewhere this weekend

1 USEFUL LANGUAGE
Making and responding to suggestions

a Complete the sentences and questions with the words in the box.

could	free	~~idea~~	let's	shall

1 That's a nice _____idea_____.
2 _____ go to that new restaurant.
3 _____ we go to the cinema?
4 I'm not _____ on Tuesday.
5 We _____ go swimming.

b Underline the correct words to complete the conversation.

ANGELA I went to the beach last week. It was great.
SUZY Oh, [1]*let / let's* go to the beach together some time!
ANGELA [2]*That's / This is* a lovely idea.
SUZY We [3]*could / shall* go this weekend.
ANGELA I'm sorry, I'm [4]*free / busy* with my family this weekend.
SUZY OK. [5]*Shall we / We shall* go next Saturday?
ANGELA I [6]*can't / don't* go on Saturday but I'm [7]*free / busy* on Sunday. I can go on Sunday.
SUZY [8]*Nice / OK*, Sunday. Good.
ANGELA Great!

c ▶ 8.6 Listen and check.

d Put the conversation in the correct order.

☐	**SAYEED**	Great! Let's go now.
☐	**SAYEED**	OK, that's a nice idea! See you at eleven.
☐	**SAYEED**	OK. We could go at eleven.
1	**SAYEED**	Shall we go for a coffee?
☐	**ANYA**	Great! Shall we go to the new Polish café?
☐	**ANYA**	Coffee? Good idea!
☐	**ANYA**	I'm sorry, I can't go now. I have a meeting at ten o'clock.

e ▶ 8.7 Listen and check.

2 PRONUNCIATION
Main stress and tone

a ▶ 8.8 Listen to the sentences. Does the tone rise (↗) or fall (↘) after the underlined main stress? Tick (✓) the correct box.

	↗	↘
1 Shall we go for a <u>meal</u> tomorrow?		✓
2 That's a <u>lovely</u> idea.		
3 Let's go to the <u>cinema</u> next week.		
4 That's a <u>great</u> idea.		
5 I'm <u>away</u> on Tuesday.		
6 That's a <u>nice</u> idea.		

8C Skills for Writing
This is to say thank you

1 READING

a Read the thank you notes. Complete the sentences with the names in the box.

~~Charlie~~ Emi Helen Nina Oscar Russell

1 ____Charlie____ helped a friend with his flat.
2 _____ drove to hospital.
3 _____ helped a friend at the shops.
4 _____ needed to go to hospital.
5 _____ bought things for his flat.
6 _____ bought a new dress.

2 WRITING SKILLS
Writing short emails, letters and notes

a <u>Underline</u> the correct words to complete the email.

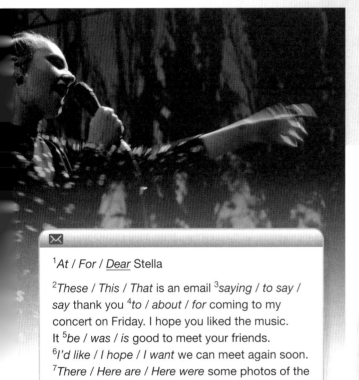

✉
¹*At / For / Dear* Stella

²*These / This / That* is an email ³*saying / to say / say* thank you ⁴*to / about / for* coming to my concert on Friday. I hope you liked the music. It ⁵*be / was / is* good to meet your friends. ⁶*I'd like / I hope / I want* we can meet again soon. ⁷*There / Here are / Here were* some photos of the evening. I like the picture of you and Ali!

Best ⁸*wishes / wish / luck*

Ava

b Match 1–6 with a–f to make expressions.

1 [d] Dear   a some photos of the party.
2 [ ] Here are   b soon.
3 [ ] Thanks for   c wishes,
4 [ ] I hope we can d Tony,
5 [ ] See you   e meet again soon.
6 [ ] Best   f your note.

Hi Emi

This is a note to say thank you for your help on Wednesday. It was fun to go shopping together and you helped me find a really nice dress. Now I need some shoes!

See you soon

Nina

Hi Charlie

This is a short email to say thanks for your help at the weekend. The new table and chairs look really good. I bought some big pictures and lamps on Monday. I hope you can come for dinner some time!

Best wishes

Russell

Hi Oscar

Here are some chocolates to say thank you for driving me to hospital on Monday. You were great! I'm home again now but in bed for a few days. I hope we can meet for a drink soon.

Best wishes

Helen

3 WRITING

a Write a thank you note to your friend Marie. Remember to give information about:

- the lunch you had at her house
- the people you met
- your photos of the day
- when you hope to meet her again.

Hi Marie

_____
_____
_____
_____
_____
_____
_____
_____
_____
_____

Best wishes

_____

UNIT 8
Reading and listening extension

1 READING

a Read the blog. Are the sentences true or false?

1 Jill was at work on Friday.
2 She lives with Mel and Amy.
3 She was in her office on Sunday.
4 She had lunch with Angela on Sunday.
5 Mel and Amy went to Dublin on Monday.
6 Jill and Angela travelled to the airport together.

b Read the blog again. <u>Underline</u> the correct words to complete the sentences.

1 Jill had a *good* / *bad* day at work on Friday.
2 She *went to the theatre* / *stayed at home* on Friday evening.
3 She missed the end of the film because she was *tired* / *bored*.
4 She *watched a cookery programme* / *cooked an Indian meal* on Sunday.
5 Angela bought *a suitcase* / *some books* on Sunday.
6 Jill and her friends had pizza for *lunch* / *dinner* on Sunday.
7 They were in the pizza restaurant for *three* / *four* hours.
8 Jill got up *early* / *late* on Monday.
9 Jill and Angela arrived in Dublin at *7:40* / *8:40* on Monday.
10 They were in Dublin *for a holiday* / *on business*.

c Write a blog about your daily life. Write about last week. Think about these questions:

- What did you do?
- Where did you go?
- Who did you see?

📅 FRIDAY 9th JAN

I had a horrible day at work. The office was really busy. I was so happy to get home. My flatmates, Mel and Amy, wanted me to go to the theatre with them, but I was tired. They went out, but I watched an old film in my bedroom. It was a brilliant murder story, but I fell asleep before the end, so I don't know who the killer was!

📅 SUNDAY 11th JAN

I got up late and had a long bath, then I watched a programme about Indian cookery. I was a bit hungry after the programme so I had cheese on toast – my favourite! I met Angela in town for lunch and then we went shopping. I bought a suitcase for our holiday in Ireland and Angela got some books. At 6:00 we met Mel and Amy for a pizza. We were in the restaurant till 10:00!

📅 MONDAY 12th JAN

I got up at 4:00 this morning. I was really tired, but our plane to Ireland was at 6:30. I went to the airport in a taxi. Angela was already there with the tickets. It only took seventy minutes to travel from London to Dublin. We had breakfast on the plane, then Angela read one of her new books and I looked out of the window. We had a tour of Dublin today, and now we're at our hotel, which is lovely!

2 LISTENING

a  ▶ 8.9 Listen to the conversation. Complete the text with the words in the box.

Barcelona   the beach   a concert   work
a restaurant   a museum   ~~home~~   the park

Matt

Matt was at ¹___home___ with his children on Saturday, but his wife was at ²_____. On Sunday, they all went to ³_____ in ⁴_____.

Grace

Grace and her sister were in ⁵_____ at the weekend. They went to ⁶_____ on ⁷_____ on Saturday and to ⁸_____ on Sunday.

b ▶ 8.9 Listen again. Who says the sentences? Write *Matt* or *Grace*.

1 I think they were a bit bored.   ___Matt___
2 ... it wasn't very cold ...   _____
3 There were a lot of people.   _____
4 The bands were very good.   _____
5 The restaurant was empty!   _____
6 A family ticket was only £10.00!   _____
7 There weren't any other people.   _____
8 It was really interesting.   _____
9 There was a lot to see and do.   _____
10 It was free.   _____

c Write an email to a friend about last weekend. Remember to say:

- where you were
- who you were with
- what you did.

1 GRAMMAR

Correct the mistakes.

1 I am in a meeting yesterday afternoon.
   I was in a meeting yesterday afternoon.
2 Emilia not was at work yesterday.
3 We are in the USA in 1996.
4 Where they were yesterday?
5 We was play tennis.
6 Jessie arrivd at nine o'clock.
7 I did have breakfast this morning.
8 Carrie goed to New York last year.

2 VOCABULARY

Tick (✓) the sentences that are correct. Correct the mistakes.

1 ☐ Where were you ago five years?
     Where were you five years ago?
2 ☐ I saw Harry the last week.
3 ☐ We had a meeting on Monday.
4 ☐ Olivia was here at the weekend.
5 ☐ They listened music last night.
6 ☐ I had a shower this morning.
7 ☐ We played computer games at the weekend.
8 ☐ We went the cinema yesterday.

↻ REVIEW YOUR PROGRESS

Look again at Review your progress on p.70 of the Student's Book. How well can you do these things now?
3 = very well   2 = well   1 = not so well

I CAN ...

talk about past events	☐
describe events in the past	☐
make and respond to suggestions.	☐

9A We didn't stay in their house

1 GRAMMAR Past simple: negative

a Underline the correct words to complete the text.

@ YOUSSEF'S PLACE, MARRAKESH

Last year we ¹*don't had / didn't have / didn't had* a holiday here in the UK. We went to Morocco. We ²*don't stayed / weren't stay / didn't stay* in a hotel – we camped at 'Youssef's place' near Marrakesh. We had a big tent with two beds. The campsite was very beautiful and there were lots of great people there. (We ³*didn't meet / didn't met / don't met* Youssef but we met his brother!)

Youssef's place isn't in Marrakesh – it's about 40 minutes from the city. We ⁴*not drove / didn't drove / didn't drive* there – we took a taxi. Marrakesh is an exciting city but we ⁵*didn't go / don't went / didn't went* there every day. We visited small towns and villages near the campsite and walked in the mountains.

The holiday wasn't expensive. The tent cost $30 a night and we usually cooked our meals in the campsite kitchen. But we ⁶*don't cook / not cooked / didn't cook* every night! We visited some great restaurants and cafés in Marrakesh.

b Complete the conversations with the past simple negative form of the verbs in brackets.

1 **A** Our father went to Los Angeles last week. He stayed in a hotel, I think.
   B No, he _didn't stay_ (stay) in a hotel. He stayed at a campsite.
2 **A** We visited a lot of museums on holiday.
   B We _____ (visit) a lot of museums. We visited two museums! That's not a lot!
3 **A** How was the café?
   B I went to the office! I _____ (go) to a café!
4 **A** They had a car on holiday in France.
   B Well, no, they _____ (have) a car. They had bikes.
5 **A** I bought a few new clothes yesterday.
   B You _____ (buy) a few new clothes! You bought a lot of new clothes!
6 **A** I read a lot of books last weekend.
   B You _____ (read) a lot of books. You read one book! That's all!

c ▶9.1 Listen and check.

2 VOCABULARY Transport

a Write the words under the pictures.

bike	~~boat~~ bus car underground	
plane	taxi train tram	

1 ____boat____   2 _____   3 _____

4 _____   5 _____   6 _____

7 _____   8 _____   9 _____

3 PRONUNCIATION

Sound and spelling: The letter *a*

a ▶9.2 Listen to the words in the box. What sound do the **marked** letters have? Complete the table.

~~what~~ taxi car flat train father take		
plane watch want camp garden		

Sound 1 /æ/ (e.g. *cat*)	Sound 2 /ɑː/ (e.g. *park*)	Sound 3 /eɪ/ (e.g. *plate*)	Sound 4 /ɒ/ (e.g. *not*)
			what

1 GRAMMAR Past simple: questions

a Put the words in the correct order to make questions.

1 last / did / go / holiday / year / on / where / you ?
Where did you go on holiday last year?

2 you / did / there / how / get ?
_____

3 go / friend / a / you / with / did ?
_____

4 stay / you / did / where ?
_____

5 up / get / what / did / you / time ?
_____

6 lot / buy / things / of / you / did / a ?
_____

7 did / beach / the / go / you / to ?
_____

8 holiday / did / enjoy / you / the ?
_____

b Complete the conversation with the words in the box.

Did he   was   ~~did~~   did he get   Did Jack stay
Did you   did you stay   he did   he didn't   I didn't

A What ¹____did____ you do at New Year? ²_____
go out?
B No, ³_____. I stayed at home.
A Really? Why ⁴_____ at home?
B I wasn't very well.
A Oh, no! ⁵_____ at home?
B No, ⁶_____. He went into the city.
A ⁷_____ see the fireworks?
B Yes, ⁸_____.
A What time ⁹_____ home?
B I don't know. I ¹⁰_____ in bed!

c ▶9.3 Listen and check.

2 VOCABULARY
The seasons and the weather

a Find the four seasons and six more weather words.

r	a	i	n	y	j	x	l	y	s
z	y	v	p	x	l	z	z	p	p
f	w	a	r	m	j	q	c	k	r
f	y	p	n	b	h	v	o	d	i
y	j	a	q	k	o	x	l	x	n
c	l	u	s	k	t	v	d	d	g
l	b	t	j	z	h	q	t	p	p
o	f	u	q	s	u	m	m	e	r
u	b	m	v	n	k	t	l	v	z
d	q	n	n	j	p	y	f	t	s
y	x	b	v	t	j	z	y	k	n
q	w	i	n	t	e	r	v	q	o
y	p	s	u	n	n	y	z	j	w

b Underline the correct words to complete the conversations.

1 **A** It's –7°C! I don't like ¹*summer* / *winter*!
  B Really? I like this season. I like ²*cloud* / *cold* weather and I really like ³*snowy* / *snow*!
2 **A** It's really ⁴*wind* / *windy* today.
  B Yes, there's always a lot of ⁵*wind* / *windy* in the autumn.
3 **A** Look at the ⁶*rain* / *rainy*!
  B I know. It often ⁷*rains* / *rainy* in this country.
4 **A** Did you have good weather on holiday? It was 42°C here.
  B 42°C! No, it wasn't ⁸*hot* / *cold* but it was ⁹*warm* / *wind* and ¹⁰*sun* / *sunny* every day.

c ▶9.4 Listen and check.

3 PRONUNCIATION
Sound and spelling: The letter o

a ▶9.5 Listen to the words in the box. What sound do the **marked** letters have? Complete the table.

~~cl**ou**d~~   h**o**t   sn**o**wy   h**o**liday   t**ow**n   c**o**ld
ph**o**ne   ag**o**   d**o**ctor   br**ow**n   wr**o**ng   tr**ou**sers

Sound 1 /əʊ/ (e.g. *no*)	Sound 2 /aʊ/ (e.g. *now*)	Sound 3 /ɒ/ (e.g. *not*)
	cloud	

9C Everyday English
Can you do something for me?

1 USEFUL LANGUAGE
Making and responding to requests

a Complete the conversations with the sentences in the box.

Sorry, I can't. I'm really busy.
Thanks, that's really kind of you.
Sure, no problem.
Can you do something for me?
Oh, OK, I'll do it then.
Could you meet me at the station on Sunday?
~~Can you go to the shops?~~

Conversation 1
A *Can you go to the shops?* We need bread.
B Sorry, I'm really busy.
A ¹_____

Conversation 2
A ²_____
B Sure, what is it?
A ³_____
B Yes, certainly.
A ⁴_____

Conversation 3
A Can you come to the shops with me today?
B ⁵_____
A Oh, OK. Could you come with me tomorrow?
B ⁶_____
A Thanks.

b ▶9.6 Listen and check.

c Put the conversation in the correct order.

	KERRY	Can you pick Jenny up from school at four?
1	KERRY	Hi, it's Kerry here.
	KERRY	See you.
	KERRY	Thanks, that's really kind of you.
	KERRY	I'm fine, thanks. Could you do something for me?
	SAL	Yes, of course. What is it?
	SAL	Sure, no problem.
	SAL	Hi Kerry, how are you?
	SAL	That's OK. See you later.

d ▶9.7 Listen and check.

2 PRONUNCIATION
Syllables and spelling

a ▶9.8 Listen to the words. How many syllables do they have? Add the words to the correct group.

~~lovely~~ ~~expensive~~ beautiful station autumn
different museum cinema restaurant
interesting holiday campsite

2 syllables	3 syllables
lovely	expensive

9C Skills for Writing
After that, we went to a party

1 READING

a Read three online posts about New Year and tick (✓) the correct people. Sometimes there is more than one possible answer.

	Jiang	Liam	Fernanda
1 Who had dinner in a restaurant?			✓
2 Who had fish for dinner?			
3 Who wore new clothes?			
4 Who met some friends?			
5 Who was with family?			
6 Who watched TV?			
7 Who cleaned the house?			
8 Who saw fireworks?			

2 WRITING SKILLS
Making the order clear

a <u>Underline</u> the correct words to complete the online post.

What did you do on your last birthday?

I'm a doctor so I was at work in the day – but the evening was fun! ¹*First that, / <u>First</u>*, my friend Tess arrived at my house with a beautiful birthday cake. ²*After, / Then*, my friend Dave phoned from New York. ³*After that, / After,* I met my sister at a Chinese restaurant and we had a very good meal.
Anita, 29   👍 1 like

For my last birthday I went to London with my friend Alan. We went on a boat on the river in the morning. It was nice but it was very cold! ⁴*First, / After that,* we had lunch and ⁵*next that, / then*, we went to a football match. Our team didn't win 😠 but we had a good time anyway!
Ricky, 20   👍 3 likes

Last year I had a really fun birthday. ⁶*First / Next*, I had lunch with my family. ⁷*After then, / Then*, I went shopping with my sister. I bought some clothes and a nice new watch. ⁸*After that, / Next time*, I met my friends Iris, Calvin and Robert. We had a drink and talked all evening.
Wendy, 21   👍 1 like

What did you do last New Year?

👤 First, my sisters and I cleaned the house. Then, we went shopping for new clothes. I bought a red dress for New Year. After that, we cooked fish, vegetables and rice for the evening meal. We had a big family New Year dinner at our home with our parents and grandparents. We didn't go out but we saw lots of fireworks near our house.
Jiang, *China*
Like | Reply | Share

👤 First, I went to my brother's flat and we watched a film. We had pizza and ice cream. It was OK. Then, we went into town and met some friends. It was very cold (I only had my old black jeans and T-shirt – no coat or hat!) but we watched the fireworks for about ten minutes. After that, I went home and watched TV.
Liam, *UK*
Like | Reply | Share

👤 First, I had dinner in a restaurant with my friends. I had fish and it was very good. After that, we went to a party on the beach. It was great! I wore a new white dress. There were lots of people on the beach. We put flowers in the water and watched the fireworks. After that, we sat and talked until about 4:00 am.
Fernanda, *Brazil*
Like | Reply | Share

3 WRITING

a What did you do last New Year? Write an online post.

👤

Like | Reply | Share

55

UNIT 9
Reading and listening extension

1 READING

a Read the web article. Match the people to the pictures 1–3.

Billy ☐   Monica ☐   Lee ☐

b Read the article again. Complete the sentences with *Billy*, *Monica* or *Lee*.

1 ___*Lee*___ travelled with a friend.
2 _____ wanted to surprise a friend.
3 _____ made a journey to find a new job.
4 _____ was on holiday.
5 _____ met an important person on a journey.
6 _____ didn't see his or her friend.
7 _____ had a problem because of the weather.
8 _____ didn't arrive in the correct city.

c Write about a journey you made. Remember to give information about:

- when the journey was
- why you made the journey
- where you travelled from and to
- what happened on the journey.

WE ASKED OUR READERS TO SEND IN THEIR TRAVEL STORIES. HERE ARE SOME OF THEM:

Billy, 35

Four years ago I went to London for a job interview. Trains are expensive in the UK, so I went by bus. The journey was about five hours. I didn't have anything to read so I started talking to the woman in the seat next to me. Her name was Milly. We got married last year and now we have a baby boy!

Monica, 27

I was in the USA on business and I had some free time, so I flew to New York to visit my friend, Chris. I didn't tell her because I wanted to surprise her. I arrived but Chris wasn't at home. The man in the flat next door said she was on holiday! I got a taxi back to the airport but it started to snow and there were no flights, so I slept at the airport. It was awful!

Lee, 20

In the university holiday, my friend and I decided to drive to Budapest for a music concert. We didn't have a map, but we didn't think it was important. The journey was fun and we arrived late at night. In the morning, we looked around the city, but it didn't look like the photos of Budapest on the Internet. After a few hours, we realised we were in Bucharest in Romania, not Budapest in Hungary!

 Review

1 GRAMMAR

Tick (✓) the past simple sentences that are correct. Correct the mistakes.

1 ☐ **A** Did you take these photos?
   B Yes, I took.
   Yes, I did.
2 ☐ Where did you go?
3 ☐ I didn't saw Sabine.
4 ☐ What time you arrived?
5 ☐ Elena didn't get up early.
6 ☐ What did they do?
7 ☐ **A** Did you visit your friends?
   B No, I didn't visit.
8 ☐ Matt didn't read his emails.

2 VOCABULARY

Correct the mistakes.

1 The weather's very cold and cloud today.
   The weather's very cold and cloudy today.
2 We took train to Milan.
3 We went with plane to Stockholm.
4 This is a photo of the snowy in the garden.
5 **A** Did you drive to the station?
   B No, we went by the bus.
6 It always rainy here in the summer.
7 Did you go with car to Moscow?
8 It was suny and warm yesterday.

2 LISTENING

a ⏵**9.9** Listen to the interview. <u>Underline</u> the correct words to complete the sentences.

1 The woman is *working* / *on holiday* today.
2 The woman *knows* / *doesn't know* the man.
3 The man and woman met *on holiday last year* / *in the street today.*
4 They talk about the *man's* / *woman's* holiday.

b ⏵**9.9** Listen again. Tick (✓) the sentences that are true. Correct the false sentences.

1 ☐ The man's last holiday was in summer.
   The man's last holiday was in autumn.
2 ☐ He went on holiday with his children.
   _____
3 ☐ They travelled by ship and train.
   _____
4 ☐ They were on holiday for two weeks.
   _____
5 ☐ They stayed in a flat near the beach.
   _____
6 ☐ It was their first visit to Portugal.
   _____
7 ☐ The man learnt some Portuguese phrases before the holiday.
   _____
8 ☐ England is often cold and rainy in autumn.
   _____

c Write a conversation between two friends talking about their last holiday. Think about these questions:
   • Where did they go?
   • How did they get there?
   • Where did they stay?
   • How was the weather?

🔄 REVIEW YOUR PROGRESS

Look again at Review your progress on p.78 of the Student's Book. How well can you do these things now?
3 = very well   2 = well   1 = not so well

I CAN ...

talk about travel and holiday experiences	☐
talk about past holidays	☐
make and respond to requests.	☐

10A I'm sitting in my flat

1 GRAMMAR
Present continuous: positive

a <u>Underline</u> the correct words to complete the text messages.

1
> *I'm cook / <u>I'm cooking</u> / I cooking* dinner. There's lots of food. Do you want to eat?

2
> Help! *Joe listening / Joe's listens / Joe's listening* to a new CD. It's really bad!

3
> I'm at the station. *It's raining / It raining / It's rain* and I don't have an umbrella. Can you meet me in the car?

4
> *We're having / We having / We're have* coffee in the Peach Tree café. See you soon.

5
> *I looking / I'm looking / I'm look* out of the window and I can see your cat. *It sitting / It's sitting / It is sit* in a tree!

b Complete the sentences with the present continuous form of the verbs in the box. Use contractions.

go ~~have~~ speak study wear work

1 They_'re having_ dinner.

2 She _____ Japanese.

3 'We _____ to school.'

4 'I _____ in the office today.'

5 He _____ a white shirt.

6 You _____ at university.

2 VOCABULARY The home

a Complete the crossword puzzle.

→ **Across**
3 'There's a shower in this room.'
4 'There's a table and six chairs in this room. We have dinner here every evening.' (6, 4)
6 'Every room has one or more. It's good to open it in hot weather.'
7 'There are lots of nice chairs in this room and a big TV.' (6, 4)
8 'Every room has one. You can walk or sit there.'

↓ **Down**
1 'There's a table and two chairs in this room. I cook and eat here.'
2 'Every room has one or two. You use it to go in or out.'
3 'I read books, listen to music, sleep and wake up in this room.'
5 'We sit here on sunny days but not on rainy days!'
6 'Every room has four or more. You can put pictures there.'

3 PRONUNCIATION
Sound and spelling: /tʃ/ and /θ/

a ▶ **10.1** Listen to the words in the box. What sound do the **marked** letters have? Complete the table.

~~bathroom~~ ki**tch**en pic**t**ure **ch**air
nin**th** mon**th** ques**ti**on **th**irty

Sound 1 /tʃ/ (e.g. *lunch*)	Sound 2 /θ/ (e.g. *bath*)
	bathroom

10B Are you working?

1 GRAMMAR Present continuous: negative and questions

a Put the words in the correct order to make sentences and questions.

1 you / are / who / phoning ?
   Who are you phoning?

2 studying / aren't / we .
   _____

3 phone / is / the / Ryan / talking / why / on ?
   _____

4 not / book / I'm / this / reading .
   _____

5 are / bus / waiting / for / friends / the / your ?
   _____

6 the / staying / hotel / isn't / at / Erica .
   _____

b ▶10.2 Listen and check.

c Complete the conversation with the present continuous form of the verbs in brackets.

ANDY Hi, it's me. Where are you? What ¹ _are you doing_ (you / do)?

TILDA I'm with Jenny and Craig.

ANDY Oh, ² _____ (you / work)?

TILDA Yes, we are. Can I have some apple juice, please?

ANDY Apple juice? What ³ _____ (you / talk) about?

TILDA Sorry, ⁴ _____ (I / not / talk) to you.
   ⁵ _____ (I / talk) to the waiter but he
   ⁶ _____ (not / listen).

ANDY Waiter? Is there a waiter at work?

TILDA No, ⁷ _____ (we / not / work) in the office.
   We're in a meeting at a café.

ANDY Oh …

d ▶10.3 Listen and check.

2 VOCABULARY Place phrases with prepositions

a Complete the sentences with *in*, *on* or *at*.

1 Is Bryan _____in_____ bed?
2 Sorry, I can't talk now. I'm _____ the airport.
3 Were you _____ school yesterday?
4 Why did you take photos _____ the plane?
5 Angie's _____ the bus stop.
6 Kay and Ellie are _____ holiday.
7 Did you read _____ the train?
8 I talked to Jason _____ the party.
9 Your bag is _____ the car.
10 I saw this film _____ the cinema last year.
11 Is there wi-fi _____ the hotel?
12 I have wi-fi _____ home.

b Underline the correct words to complete the conversations.

1 **A** Where are you? Are you _at_ / in / on the airport?
   B No, I'm at / in / on the cinema! It's a really good film!
2 **A** Is Pasha at / in / on work?
   B No, he's at / in / on holiday.
3 **A** You could phone Stella. She's at / in / on home.
   B I don't have my phone. It's at / in / on the car.
4 **A** Is Allie at / in / on school?
   B No, she's at / in / on bed.
5 **A** Are you at / in / on the bus?
   B No, there aren't any buses. I'm at / in / on a taxi.
6 **A** I'm still at / in / on the station. The train's late.
   B Oh dear. Can you phone when you're at / in / on the train?

c ▶10.4 Listen and check.

3 PRONUNCIATION Sound and spelling: /ə/

a ▶10.5 Listen and underline the /ə/ sound in each word.

1 husb**a**nd
2 picture
3 Brazil
4 daughter
5 autumn
6 ago
7 Japanese
8 hospital
9 computer
10 afternoon

1 USEFUL LANGUAGE
Asking for travel information

a Complete the expressions with the words in the box.

| four o'clock office train ~~six~~ stop ten minutes |

1 platform _six_
2 ticket _____
3 direct _____
4 in _____
5 at _____
6 bus _____

b Complete the conversation with the words in the box.

| at can bus stop direct change |
| ~~excuse~~ help problem next ticket |

A Oh ¹_____excuse_____ me!
B Yes? How ²_____ I help?
A What time's the ³_____ bus to Bath?
B It's ⁴_____ 11:15.
A So it leaves in ten minutes. Is it a ⁵_____ bus?
B No, you ⁶_____ at Bristol.
A OK, and which ⁷_____ is it?
B Number 2, near the ⁸_____ office.
A Great! Thanks for your ⁹_____.
B No ¹⁰_____.

c ▶10.6 Listen and check.

d Put the conversation in the correct order.

☐ **B** No problem.
☐ **B** Yes? How can I help?
☐ **B** No, you change at Brighton.
[1] **A** Excuse me.
☐ **A** What time's the next train to Eastbourne?
☐ **B** The next train leaves in half an hour.
☐ **A** So at 10:25. Is it a direct train?
☐ **B** It's platform 9.
☐ **A** OK, and which platform is it?
☐ **A** Great! Thanks for your help.

e ▶10.7 Listen and check.

2 PRONUNCIATION
Sound and spelling: /ɪə/ and /eə/

a ▶10.8 Listen to the words in the box. What sound do the **marked** letters have? Complete the table.

| ~~pair~~ wear we're meal there |
| year here chair where clear |

Sound 1 /ɪə/ (e.g. *hear*)	Sound 2 /eə/ (e.g. *hair*)
	pair

1 READING

a Read the messages. Are the sentences true or false?

1 Sol and Eliana are at the cinema.
2 Joel wants information about the film and the cinema.
3 Sian is walking in the rain.
4 Sian needs information about a football game and a concert.
5 Basek isn't driving to the station.
6 Basek has a ticket for the train.

2 WRITING SKILLS
Word order in questions

a Complete the questions. Write one word in each gap.

1 **A** How much ___were___ ___the___ ___tickets___?
  B The tickets were £2.50.
2 **A** _____ _____ _____ late?
  B Yes, the train's late.
3 **A** He's going home.
  B Why _____ _____ _____ home?
4 **A** Where _____ _____ _____ this T-shirt?
  B I didn't buy this T-shirt – my brother gave it to me.
5 **A** What time _____ _____ _____ _____?
  B The film starts at 4:45 pm.
6 **A** Where _____ I _____ a taxi?
  B You can get a taxi outside the station.
7 **A** _____ _____ _____ _____ restaurant?
  B Yes, it's an expensive restaurant.
8 **A** _____ _____ _____ _____ a car park?
  B Yes, the hotel has a car park.

b Put the words in the correct order to make questions.

1 from / you / are / where ?
  Where are you from?
2 on / Nick / playing / the / computer / is ?
  _____
3 have / their / how / does / flat / rooms / many ?
  _____
4 the / yesterday / give / any / did / teacher / homework / us ?
  _____
5 can / where / ticket / a / bus / buy / I ?
  _____
6 he / school / today / at / was ?
  _____

Hi Sol, I'm having lunch with Eliana and she'd like to come to the cinema with us tomorrow. Sorry, I can't remember two things. What time does the film start? And which cinema is it? Thanks, Joel

SEND

Hi Brandon, It's a lovely day here today – very cold but sunny. I'm walking to the shops and I want to buy something for Gabriel. Can you tell me two things? Does he like football? And what sort of music does he like? Thanks, Sian

SEND

Hi Catalina, I'm late for the train but I'm in a taxi. Two questions: do you have my train ticket or do I need to buy a ticket? Which platform does the train leave from? See you soon! Basek

SEND

3 WRITING

a Write a message to another student about your new English class. Remember to ask about:

• the classroom
• the time of the class
• the homework.

SEND

UNIT 10
Reading and listening extension

1 READING

a Read the email. Tick (✓) the sentences that are true. Correct the false sentences.

1 ☐ Jenny is on holiday in Germany.
   Jenny is on holiday in Japan.
2 ☐ Anna is studying German.
   _____
3 ☐ There are three people in the German family.
   _____
4 ☐ Today is Saturday.
   _____
5 ☐ Anna is in the bedroom at the moment.
   _____
6 ☐ Most people in the family are outside now.
   _____
7 ☐ Anna wants to know what Martin is doing.
   _____

b Read the email again. <u>Underline</u> the correct words to complete the sentences.

1 *Jenny / Anna / <u>Anna's parents</u>* organised Anna's course in Hamburg.
2 It's a *one / two / three* week course.
3 Anna is staying in a *hotel / house / flat* in Germany.
4 Anna doesn't always *hear / understand / listen to* what the family say to her.
5 *Martin / Ralf / Karl* isn't inside the house at the moment.
6 Ralf is *studying / playing a game / texting his friends*.
7 Andrea is *relaxing / working / helping Martin*.
8 Anna doesn't like Martin's *children / food / music*.

c Write a description of an evening in your home. Remember to give information about:

- who is in your home
- where each person is
- what each person is doing.

Hi Jenny,

Thanks for your email. I hope you're enjoying your holiday in Japan. I'm in Hamburg in Germany for two weeks. Mum and Dad sent me here to do a German course. I didn't really want to come!

I'm staying with a German family here. The parents are Martin and his wife, Andrea, and they have two sons, Karl and Ralf. Karl is 17 and Ralf is 14. They're very friendly but they only speak German and sometimes I don't understand them.

It's Sunday and everyone is at home, but we're all in different parts of the house. I'm writing this email in my bedroom. It's really nice because I can see the garden from my window. Karl is in the garden. It's raining but he's playing with the dog. Ralf is in the room next to me. His parents think he is studying for his exams, but he's playing a computer game and chatting to his friends online.

Andrea is in the living room. She's a teacher and she's preparing her lessons for next week. Martin is cooking dinner and listening to some terrible opera music. I don't know what he's making, but he's a great cook. My dad can only make toast!

Anyway, what are you doing? Write and let me know.

Anna

2 LISTENING

a ▶10.9 Listen. Complete the sentences with the names in the box.

| Jack Mum Melinda Dad Tim |

1 _____Jack_____ is at home.
2 _____ is at work.
3 _____ is at the sports centre.
4 _____ and _____ are at the train station.

b ▶10.9 Listen again. Underline the correct words to complete the sentences.

1 Jack's dad is *working in* / *phoning* his office.
2 Jack is *at home* / *at the cinema*.
3 Jack is *watching TV* / *listening to music*.
4 Melinda and her friends *are* / *aren't* at Melinda's house.
5 Jack's mum is with *her husband* / *one of her sons*.
6 Tim isn't wearing a *coat* / *jumper*.
7 It's beginning to *snow* / *rain*.
8 The station *is* / *isn't* busy.

c You are somewhere in your home town. Write a phone conversation between you and a friend. Remember to say:
- where you are
- what you are doing
- what is happening around you.

⊙ Review

1 GRAMMAR

Correct the mistakes.

1 I driving to the hospital.
 I'm driving to the hospital.
2 She don't working today.
3 You having lunch?
4 Where Vicky going?
5 They're siting in the garden.
6 It raining?
7 No, it not.
8 Yes, is.

2 VOCABULARY

Tick (✓) the sentences that are correct. Correct the mistakes.

1 ☐ Is Jasper in the livving room?
  Is Jasper in the living room?
2 ☐ Cheryl's on holiday.
3 ☐ I'm in the kitchin.
4 ☐ Jerry's at home.
5 ☐ Amber's on the bus.
6 ☐ They're in the dinning room.
7 ☐ She's at a party.
8 ☐ George isn't at bed.
9 ☐ I'm at airport.
10 ☐ We're on a taxi.

⟳ REVIEW YOUR PROGRESS

Look again at Review your progress on p.86 of the Student's Book. How well can you do these things now?
3 = very well   2 = well   1 = not so well

I CAN ...

talk about my home	☐
ask where people are and what they're doing	☐
ask for travel information.	☐

1 GRAMMAR Object pronouns

a Underline the correct words.

1 Where are the tickets? I had *they* / <u>*them*</u> a minute ago.
2 *We* / *Us* like Joel a lot. He's staying with *we* / *us* at the moment.
3 This is my sister. *Me* / *I* phone *her* / *she* every day.
4 I was on TV. Did you see *I* / *me*?
5 Where's my umbrella? I need *her* / *it*!
6 That man's playing tennis really well. *Him* / *He* is very good. Look at *him* / *he*!
7 **A** Bye, John! Bye, Bev! See *you* / *them* tomorrow!
  B OK! Bye!

b Complete the conversation with subject and object pronouns.

A [1]_____ 've got some photos of the party.
  [2]_____ 're very funny.
B Oh, can I see [3]_____?
A Yes, just a minute … OK … My brother's in this picture.
  [4]_____ arrived very late.
B Really? Where is [5]_____? I can't see
  [6]_____!
A [7]_____'s there, with the green hat!
B Oh yes! [8]_____'s a very big hat! Is that
  [9]_____? It's your T-shirt.
A Yes, that's [10]_____. I'm with Ian and Debbie.
  [11]_____'re really nice.
B And who's that?
A That's Anna-Maria. [12]_____'s at our house at the
  moment. [13]_____'s staying with [14]_____.
B Can I meet [15]_____?
A Yes, of course. [16]_____ really wants to meet
  [17]_____!

c ▶ 11.1 Listen and check.

2 VOCABULARY Life events

a Write the words under the pictures.

| be born   die   finish school   finish university   ~~get married~~ |
| go to university   grow up   have a baby   stop working |

1 _get married_   2 _____   3 _____

4 _____   5 _____   6 _____

7 _____   8 _____   9 _____

b <u>Underline</u> the correct words to complete the text.

Liliana, Rosa and me

Liliana [1]<u>*was*</u> / *is* born on 1 January 1960 in a small town in Colombia. Her family didn't have much money but they were very happy. Liliana [2]*got to* / *went to* school until she was 16, then she got a job in an office. She met her husband, Andreas, there. They [3]*got* / *had* a baby girl and they called her Rosa.

Time passed and Rosa grew [4]*on* / *up*. She finished [5]*the school* / *school* and went to [6]*the university* / *university* in the USA. She often visited her parents but she didn't live with them again. Then, sadly, Andreas [7]*stopped* / *died*. He was only 46. Liliana was very sad and she [8]*ended* / *stopped* working.

Three years ago, she came to the USA to be with Rosa. I started a conversation with Liliana on a train one day and two weeks later I met her daughter, Rosa. Rosa and I [9]*got* / *went* married in June!

3 PRONUNCIATION
Sound and spelling: /ɜː/

a ▶ 11.2 Listen and <u>underline</u> the word which DOESN'T have the /ɜː/ sound.

1	work	<u>sport</u>	shirt
2	daughter	thirty	Thursday
3	university	early	near
4	born	first	world
5	people	person	girl
6	Turkish	grow	weren't

11B She can pull a plane

1 GRAMMAR can

a Underline the correct words to complete the sentences and questions.

1 Your pictures are beautiful! You *can* / *can't* paint very well.
2 **A** *You can* / *Can you* cook?
  B Yes, *can I* / *I can*.
3 I like music but I *can't* / *can* dance at all! I'm a terrible dancer!
4 Jenny *can to* / *can* speak German very well.
5 **A** *Can he* / *Cans he* run 10 km?
  B No, he *can't* / *doesn't*.
6 They're good swimmers. They *can swim very well* / *can very well swim*.

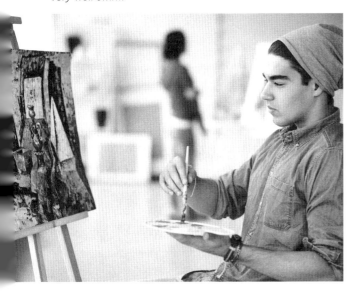

b ▶11.3 Listen and check.

c Complete the sentences with *can* or *can't* and a verb from the box.

drive	play	read	say	~~speak~~	swim	teach	write

1 James __can speak__ Italian quite well.
2 He goes to the beach every day but he never goes in the water because he _____.
3 Their daughter is only four but she _____ books.
4 _____ you _____ a car?
5 I like children but I _____ them. I'm not a teacher.
6 Listen to this! We _____ 'Hello' in Chinese.
7 Look at this! I _____ 'Hello' in Russian.
8 I'd like to have guitar lessons. I often listen to guitar music but I _____ the guitar at all.

2 VOCABULARY Abilities

a Match 1–8 to a–h to make questions.

1 [f] Can you ride   a in the sea in your country?
2 [ ] When did you last paint   b dance?
3 [ ] How often do you cook   c a meal for lots of people?
4 [ ] You're at a party and you d 5 km?
   like the music. Do you   e a picture?
5 [ ] Did you sing   f a horse?
6 [ ] Can you run   g a song yesterday?
7 [ ] Do people swim   h a car?
8 [ ] How often do you drive

b ▶11.4 Listen and check.

c Complete the crossword puzzle with past simple verbs.

```
 1 S  a  n  g
 2 [ ][ ][ ]      3 [ ]      4 [ ]
                        5 [ ]
        6 [ ][ ]
           7 [ ][ ][ ][ ]
 8 [ ][ ][ ][ ][ ]
```

→ **Across**
1 In the evening we sat outside and s__ang_____ songs.
2 I p_____ basketball every day when I was at school.
6 We r_____ 5 km in the park this morning.
7 Ellie c_____ dinner yesterday. It was very good.
8 Gino p_____ a picture of the flowers in the garden.

↓ **Down**
1 I only s_____ for five minutes because the water was very cold!
3 The music was really good and we d_____ all night.
4 Damian r_____ his bicycle to school every day last week.
5 I d_____ our new car for the first time yesterday.

3 PRONUNCIATION Sentence stress: *can*

a ▶11.5 Listen to the sentences. Which words are stressed? Tick (✓) the correct box.

1 a [ ] I <u>can</u> swim.   4 a [ ] <u>Jim can't sing</u>.
  b [✓] I can <u>swim</u>.   b [ ] Jim can't <u>sing</u>.
2 a [ ] <u>Can you</u> drive?   5 a [ ] Can he <u>dance</u>?
  b [ ] Can you <u>drive</u>?   b [ ] <u>Can he</u> dance?
3 a [ ] <u>Yes</u>, I can.   6 a [ ] <u>No</u>, he <u>can't</u>.
  b [ ] Yes, I <u>can</u>.   b [ ] No, <u>he</u> can't.

1 USEFUL LANGUAGE
Talking about opinions

a Complete the sentences and questions with the words in the box.

idea	agree	right	nice	~~so~~	think

1 I don't think _____so_____.
2 Maybe you're _____.
3 I don't think it's a good _____.
4 I think it's very _____.
5 What do you _____?
6 Yes, I _____.

b <u>Underline</u> the correct words to complete the conversations.

Conversation 1

A [1]*What* / *How* do you think of this room?
B I don't [2]*think* / *agree* grey is a good idea for the walls.
A [3]*You're maybe* / *Maybe you're* right. But [4]*I* / *I'm* think it's OK with the red bed.
B I'm not [5]*so* / *right* sure.

Conversation 2

A What [6]*are* / *did* you think of the film?
B It was terrible!
C Yes, [7]*I agree* / *I'm agree*. It's a really bad film!
A Really? I don't [8]*think so* / *think*. I liked it.

c ▶ **11.6** Listen and check.

d Complete the conversation with one word in each gap. A contraction, e.g. *I'm* = one word.

MARK What do you [1]____think____ of my new car?
CARRIE I [2]_____ it's really nice.
PHILIP I'm not [3]_____ sure.
CARRIE Why not?
PHILIP I [4]_____ think yellow is a very good colour.
MARK Maybe you're [5]_____.
PHILIP Mm.
MARK What [6]_____ you think of my old car?

e ▶ **11.7** Listen and check.

2 PRONUNCIATION Consonant groups

a ▶ **11.8** Listen to the words with the same consonant sound. Complete the missing letters to spell the words.

1 touri s t   s t ay
2 e _ _ ineer   e _ _ oy
3 an _ _ er   da _ _ e
4 _ _ _ ool   a _ _
5 thi _ _   ba _ _
6 liste _ _ _   fi _ _
7 clo _ _ _   si _
8 i _ _ eresting   pai _ _

1 READING

a Read the email. Tick (✓) the correct answers.

1 What's Yaz doing in Bristol?
a ☐ She's working and studying.
b ✓ She's studying.
c ☐ She's working.

2 What does Yaz think of Bristol?
a ☐ She likes it but she thinks it's expensive.
b ☐ She doesn't like it.
c ☐ She likes it because it isn't expensive.

3 Why is Yaz in Bristol?
a ☐ She's learning to play volleyball.
b ☐ She's learning to dance.
c ☐ She's studying IT.

4 What can Simon do?
a ☐ He can speak other languages.
b ☐ He can dance.
c ☐ He can speak other languages and dance.

5 Where did Yaz and Annette meet?
a ☐ They met in a bookshop.
b ☐ They met at a volleyball match.
c ☐ They met in an IT lesson.

6 How is Yaz feeling?
a ☐ She's happy because she isn't at home.
b ☐ She's having a good time but she misses people at home.
c ☐ She's very sad because she misses her friends and family.

Hi Gerhard,

Thanks for your email – it was good to hear from you.

I started university here in Bristol six weeks ago now and it's going really well. The university's fantastic and Bristol's an exciting city. It's also an expensive city. I'd like to find a job in a shop next year because I really need some money!

As you know, I'm studying IT. It's a very interesting course and the teachers are good. There's lots of work to do but there are also lots of things to do in my free time. I'm learning to dance and I can now play volleyball quite well.

I'm making some new friends here. Simon and Annette are really nice. I met Simon at my dance class. He's a language student and he can speak Italian and German very well. He's also a good dancer and he helps me in the lessons. Annette is studying IT and we met in the university bookshop on the first day. We often study together in the evening.

The people here are really nice, but I miss my family at home and I miss my friends too.

Write again soon!

Best wishes,

Yaz

2 WRITING SKILLS Pronouns

a Read the email. Change the words in brackets for subject and object pronouns.

◄ Inbox

Hi Masha,

Thank you very much for your long emails! I read ¹ _____them_____ (*your long emails*) in a café every morning. I like the photos, too. ² _____ (*The photos*) are very funny!

Things here in Rome are going well. ³ _____ (*Rome's*) a big city with lots of beautiful places to visit. I study every day and my Italian is quite good now. My language school is called Accademia Leonardo. ⁴ _____ (*Accademia Leonardo's*) a very big school but the classes are small and the teachers are great. My teacher is called Maria. ⁵ _____ (*Maria's*) very good and I like ⁶ _____ (*Maria*) very much.

I have a new friend called Luigi. He's from Venice. I met ⁷ _____ (*Luigi*) at a museum! We started talking about the pictures and then ⁸ _____ (*Luigi and I*) went for a coffee together.

How are you? Do you see Jess and Otto? I miss ⁹ _____ (*Jess and Otto*) a lot. And I miss ¹⁰ _____ (*Masha*) too, of course!

Write again soon,

Abigail

3 WRITING

a Write an email to a friend. Remember to give information about:

- where you are now
- where you study English
- your teacher
- the other students in your class
- what you do in the evening.

Hi

Write soon!

UNIT 11
Reading and listening extension

1 READING

a Read the TV review. Tick (✓) the parts of Beth's life you read about.

1 her family   ✓
2 her house   ☐
3 her school   ☐
4 her work   ☐
5 her interests   ☐
6 her husband's work   ☐
7 the death of her husband   ☐
8 her children   ☐
9 her friends   ☐

b Read the review again. Put the events in Beth's life in the order they happened.

☐ Her husband died.
☐ She had a baby.
☐ She went to South Africa.
☐ She finished her university studies.
☐ She started teaching.
☐ She got married.
1 She left Wales.
☐ She got a job in London.

c Choose an interesting member of your family and write about his or her life. Remember to give information about:

- where and when the person was born
- where the person lived
- what work the person did
- the person's family
- why the person was interesting.

LAST NIGHT'S 📺 TV

People's Lives is a popular TV programme on Channel 12. The programme helps people find out about their family history.

Last night, the programme was about Fiona Davies and her grandmother, Beth. Fiona didn't know her grandmother well because Beth died when Fiona was two years old. *People's Lives* found out that Beth was from Cardiff in Wales. She was born there in 1922 and had six brothers and sisters. The family was poor and Beth went to England when she was 17. She got a job in a hospital in London.

Beth worked at the hospital for six years, then she studied at university to be a doctor. She was 32 when she finished university and 33 when she married Fiona's grandfather, James. James was a businessman from Manchester.

Beth and James were very happy for three years and they had a son, but then James died.

Beth left the UK and went to South Africa on a ship with her son. She worked as a doctor there and started a hospital for women. In 1972, Beth returned to Cardiff to teach at the university. She taught students who wanted to be doctors. Beth died in Wales in 1984.

It was an interesting programme and Fiona was very happy to know more about her grandmother. Next week it is the turn of Frank Kendal to find out about his grandparents. Don't forget to watch!

- *People's Lives*, 8 pm next Wednesday, Channel 12

1 GRAMMAR

Correct the mistakes.

1 I've got some eggs. We can have it for breakfast.
   I've got some eggs. We can have them for breakfast.
2 Your dad's an engineer. We could ask her for help.
3 Is your phone new? I like him.
4 Your sister's really nice. How often do you see them?
5 He can to ride a horse.
6 You can drive?
7 I not can sing.
8 **A** Can they swim?
   B Yes, they swim.

2 VOCABULARY

Correct the mistakes.

1 Anita and Frank had baby in March.
   Anita and Frank had a baby in March.
2 I born in 1995.
3 She was died in 2002.
4 I finished at university last year.
5 I grew in a small village in Scotland.
6 My father stopped to work last year.
7 She singed a song last week.
8 I rode the car to the station.
9 I run 10 km last Saturday.
10 We swim in the new swimming pool yesterday.

2 LISTENING

a ▶**11.9** Listen to the conversation. Put the jobs in the order that you hear them.

- ☐ chef
- ☐ English teacher
- ☐ receptionist
- ☐ 1 singer
- ☐ tour guide

b ▶**11.9** Listen again. Tick (✓) the things that Lyn can do.

1 sing ☐
2 cook ☑
3 swim ☐
4 speak a foreign language ☐
5 teach ☐
6 speak English ☐
7 drive ☐

c ▶**11.9** Listen again. Underline the correct words.

1 Alex and Lyn are *at work* / *at home*.
2 Lyn works in *a shop* / *an office* now.
3 *Alex* / *Lyn* wants to find a new job.
4 Alex mentions *one job* / *two jobs* on a ship.
5 Lyn speaks English and *French* / *Spanish*.
6 Lyn doesn't want to live in a very *hot* / *cold* country.
7 Lyn *knows* / *doesn't know* a lot about Oxford.
8 Lyn decides to apply for the job in *Madrid* / *Oxford*.

d Write a conversation between two friends. One person describes a job he or she would like to do. The other person asks questions. Remember to say:

- what the job is
- why he or she wants to do this job
- why he or she is a good person for this job.

⊘ REVIEW YOUR PROGRESS

Look again at Review your progress on p.94 of the Student's Book. How well can you do these things now?
3 = very well   2 = well   1 = not so well

I CAN ...

talk about people's lives	☐
talk about things I know how to do	☐
talk about opinions.	☐

1 GRAMMAR

going to: positive and negative

a <u>Underline</u> the correct words to complete the conversations.

Conversation 1

A Is there an email from Stephen? [1]*He going to / He's going to / He's going* write to you with information about the boat trip.

B I don't know. [2]*I'm going not to / I'm not going to / I'm not going* check my emails today or tomorrow.

A Oh, OK. Well, I'm going [3]*to phone / phoning / phone* him this evening, so I can ask him then.

Conversation 2

A It's the holidays! [4]*I go to / I'm going / I'm going to* sleep for ten hours every night! [5]*I going / I'm going / I'm go* to watch TV every day!

B Really? That's so boring! My brother and I [6]*am going / is going / are going* to work on a farm near the mountains. The people there [7]*are going / is going / am going* to teach us how to ride horses.

A Hmm, sounds quite interesting. What about your sister?

B [8]*She's going not / She not going / She isn't going* to come with us. She wants to stay at home.

b ▶️**12.1** Listen and check.

c Complete the sentences with the *going to* form of the verbs in the box.

cook   do   have   ~~play~~   (not) ride
(not) sing   (not) stay   (not) use   watch

1 We ___are going to play___ volleyball tomorrow.
2 My sister _____ dinner for me this evening.
3 I _____ a song!
4 Samantha _____ yoga this afternoon.
5 They _____ in expensive hotels.
6 George _____ his motorbike fast.
7 I _____ a long, hot bath.
8 We _____ a film on TV this evening.
9 You _____ your phone in the restaurant!

2 VOCABULARY
Months and future time expressions

a Tick (✓) the correct ending for the sentences.

1 They're going to get married …
   a ☐ on June.   b ☐ June.   c ✓ in June.
2 It's Jim's birthday …
   a ☐ in Friday.   b ☐ this Friday.   c ☐ at Friday.
3 It's my birthday …
   a ☐ Friday.   b ☐ next Friday.   c ☐ in Friday.
4 See you …
   a ☐ in Monday.   b ☐ at Monday.
   c ☐ on Monday.
5 Can you phone me …
   a ☐ this afternoon?   b ☐ on afternoon?
   c ☐ next afternoon?
6 He's going to finish school …
   a ☐ in three weeks.   b ☐ this three weeks.
   c ☐ on three weeks.
7 See you …
   a ☐ on tomorrow.   b ☐ tomorrow.
   c ☐ in tomorrow.
8 We're going to visit Harry and Ahmed …
   a ☐ at the weekend.   b ☐ in the weekend.
   c ☐ the weekend.
9 See you …
   a ☐ at the autumn!   b ☐ on the autumn!
   c ☐ in the autumn!
10 She's going to stop working …
   a ☐ in month.   b ☐ at month.
   c ☐ next month.

3 VOCABULARY Ordinal numbers

a ▶️**12.2** Listen and write the ordinal numbers.

1st	_first_	5th	_____	16th	_____
2nd	_____	9th	_____	20th	_____
3rd	_____	12th	_____	22nd	_____
4th	_____	13th	_____	31st	_____

4 PRONUNCIATION
Sentence stress: *going to*

a ▶️**12.3** Listen and <u>underline</u> the stressed words in the sentences.

1 You're going to <u>stay</u> in a <u>hotel</u>.
2 They're going to live in Russia.
3 Anna's going to do her homework.
4 I'm going to check my emails.
5 He's going to listen to music.
6 I'm going to read a book.

1 GRAMMAR *going to*: questions

a Put the words in the correct order to make questions.

1 coffee / to / meet / when / are / we / going / for ?
When are we going to meet for coffee?

2 at / lunch / to / is / going / home / have / he ?
_____

3 where / married / to / get / going / they / are ?
_____

4 you / station / to / to / are / the / drive / tomorrow / going ?
_____

5 to / do / she / evening / going / this / what's ?
_____

6 going / potatoes / you / how / are / cook / to / the ?
_____

b ▶12.4 Listen and check.

c Complete the sentences with the *going to* form of the verbs in brackets.

1 **A** What *are you going to do* (you / do) this morning?
  B I _____ (clean) the house – and you _____ (help) me!

2 **A** So, _____ (he / play) the piano this evening?
  B Yes, he is. _____ (you / listen)?

3 **A** What _____ (you and your friends / do) in the holidays?
  B I don't know. We _____ (talk) about it this afternoon.

4 **A** Where _____ (she / watch) TV?
  B In the living room, I think.

5 When _____ (I / do) all these things on my list?

d ▶12.5 Listen and check.

2 VOCABULARY
Common verbs and collocations

a Match 1–8 with a–h to make sentences.

1 [h] I'm going to make   a my homework today.
2 [ ] I'm not going to do   b shopping tomorrow.
3 [ ] I want to clean   c Violet in hospital.
4 [ ] I'd like to paint   d a picture of you.
5 [ ] We can go   e the car. It's really dirty.
6 [ ] I don't use   f to the party.
7 [ ] I'm going to visit   g my phone every day.
8 [ ] We're going to invite Carlos h a cake for my mum.

b Complete the crossword puzzle.

→ **Across**

5 I didn't paint my r_____. I just cleaned it.
6 I need to u_____ the Internet.
7 I'd like to g_____ for a walk this afternoon.
8 Where are your dirty clothes? I'm going to do the w_____.
10 They went to the UK but they didn't v_____ London.
11 I'm going to m_____ some coffee. Would you like some?

↓ **Down**

1 I did my h*omework* this morning – English, Maths and German.
2 I'm going to c_____ the flat today. It's very dirty. I need lots of hot water!
3 I d_____ sport every day – tennis, running, swimming, football …
4 I use the c_____ every day – for email, for work, for games and for music.
9 I'm going to i_____ Pedro to my flat for lunch next week.

3 PRONUNCIATION
Sound and spelling: /v/ and /w/

a ▶12.6 Listen to the words in the box. Do they have the /v/ sound or the /w/ sound? Complete the table.

~~wall~~ evening wi-fi visit November volleyball
warm drive windy winter weekend invite

Sound 1 /v/	Sound 2 /w/
	wall

12C Everyday English
Would you like to come for dinner?

1 USEFUL LANGUAGE
Making and accepting invitations

a Put the conversation in the correct order.

- [ ] **B** Yes, I am.
- [ ] **B** Yes, I'd love to. Thank you.
- [ ] **B** I'd love to, but I have lots of homework for tomorrow.
- [ ] **A** Would you like to go to the cinema?
- [ ] **A** You're a good student! Are you free tomorrow night?
- [1] **A** Would you like to go to a concert this evening?

b ▶12.7 Listen and check.

c Put the conversation in the correct order.

- [1] **A** Would you like to come for dinner tomorrow night?
- [ ] **A** Great! You can come on Saturday.
- [ ] **A** Are you free on Friday?
- [ ] **B** No, sorry, I'm busy on Friday too. But Saturday's OK.
- [ ] **B** Thank you!
- [ ] **B** Sorry, I'm busy then.

d ▶12.8 Listen and check.

e Complete the conversations with the words in the box.

can   come   would   free   busy
~~like~~   thank   OK   love   to

Conversation 1
A Would you ¹___like___ to come to my party on Saturday?
B I'd ²_____ to come. Thank you.

Conversation 2
A ³_____ you like to go to the cinema on Thursday?
B Sorry, I'm ⁴_____ then. But Friday's ⁵_____.
A OK, we ⁶_____ go on Friday.
B Great!

Conversation 3
A Would you like to ⁷_____ for lunch at the weekend?
B I'd love ⁸_____, but I'm away this weekend.
A Are you ⁹_____ next weekend?
B Yes, I am.
A You can come then!
B ¹⁰_____ you. I'd love to come.

f ▶12.9 Listen and check.

2 PRONUNCIATION
Sound and spelling: *oo*

a ▶12.10 Listen to the words in the box. What sound do the letters *oo* have? Complete the table.

~~book~~   pool   good   school   food
boots   cook   look   afternoon

Sound 1 /uː/ (e.g. *soon*)	Sound 2 /ʊ/ (e.g. *foot*)
	book

1 READING

a Read the invitations and replies. Are the sentences true or false?

1 Eddy and Dom are going to have pizza together this evening
2 Eddy is going to make the pizza.
3 They're going to speak on the phone at 2:30 this afternoon.
4 Dom is free at 7:30 this evening.
5 Nerissa wants to go shopping in town on Tuesday morning.
6 Clare and Nerissa are going to meet this Tuesday.
7 Clare can go to Nerissa's flat this Wednesday.
8 Clare can go to Nerissa's flat next Wednesday.

Hi Dom

How are you? I'm in town this evening. Would you like to meet – at about 6:30? We could go for a meal. There's a new pizza place near the station. People say it's very good.

I can call you this afternoon – about 2:30. Is that OK with you?

Speak later,

Eddy

Hi Eddy

I'm good, thanks. Yes, I'd love to go for a pizza this evening – but I'm busy at 6:30. Is 7:30 OK for you?

I'm going to be at work this afternoon, but we could speak at about 5:30.

Dom

Hi Clare

Would you like to come to my flat on Tuesday morning? We could do some online clothes shopping together and I can make lunch.

Best wishes

Nerissa

Hi Nerissa

That's a really lovely idea but I'm staying with friends this week and I'm away until Friday. Maybe we could do it next Tuesday? I'm free next Wednesday, too.

Clare

2 WRITING SKILLS Paragraphs

a Put the paragraphs in the correct order to make Ethan's email invitation.

☐ Paul's staying with me this week and he can play the guitar really well. We could eat and then sing songs. What do you think? Are you free on Saturday?

☐ I hope you can come!

☐ Hi Jerry,

☐ I'm thinking about having a barbecue in the garden on Saturday evening – chicken, fish, vegetables, things like that. Would you and Ada like to come?

☐ Ethan

b Put the paragraphs in the correct order to make Jerry's reply to Ethan's email invitation.

☐ Is 8:00 OK? Would you like us to bring some food?

☐ Jerry

☐ See you on Saturday!

☐ Thank you, that would be lovely. We're busy on Saturday afternoon but we can come in the evening.

☐ Hi Ethan

3 WRITING

a Write a reply to the invitation.

Hi

How are you? I'm going to drive to the beach in my new car this Saturday. Would you like to come with me? We can swim, sit in the sun and play volleyball.

We could go in the morning or the afternoon. What do you think? Maybe Oliver and Jorges would like to come, too.

Simon

Hi

NEW YEAR NEW NEW ME

🗨 NEW YEAR, NEW ME
BY MATT SIMPSON

1 Today is January 1st – a good day to start my new life! Some people talk about changing their lives, but they don't do anything. I'm not going to talk about changing my life. I have a list of things I want to do and I'm going to do all of them.

2 What am I going to do first? Well, I usually get up, go to work, come home, have dinner and then watch TV until it's time to go to bed. I never do any sport. From tomorrow, I'm going to get up early every day and go for a run. I'm also going to use the swimming pool at the gym after work.

3 I'm not going to stay at home every evening. I'm going to visit the college and get some information about language courses. I'm interested in Japanese. I also want to do a cookery class. I don't know how to cook and I just eat in restaurants or buy pizzas. At the weekend, I go home to my mum for meals!

4 I spend a lot of money on clothes, but I'm not going to buy any more. I'm going to put the money in the bank. My girlfriend and I want to travel and see new places. We're planning to leave our jobs in September and travel around the world.

5 Those are my plans. What are YOU going to do to change your life this year?

1 READING

a Read the blog. Match the ideas a–e to paragraphs 1–5.

a ☐ Travelling to new places
b ☐ Asking about another person's plans
c ☐ Learning new things
d ☐ Deciding to change
e ☐ Changing a daily routine

b Read the blog again. Tick (✓) the activities Matt is going to do.

1 buy more clothes	☐	7 learn to cook	☐
2 cook a meal for his mum	☐	8 play football at the gym	☐
3 do a lot of travelling	☐	9 run every day	☐
4 get a new job	☐	10 save money	☐
5 use the gym	✓	11 study a foreign language	☐
6 learn to swim	☐	12 walk to work every day	☐

c Imagine it's a new year and you want to change your life. Make a list of things you're going to do and things you aren't going to do.

Things you're going to do	Things you aren't going to do

2 LISTENING

a ⏵ **12.11** Listen to the video call. Match the activities with the people. Complete the notes.

have dinner	meet friends	play tennis	read a book
see a football match	go to the cinema		
spend a day at Disneyland	take the dog for a walk		
~~visit a film studio~~			

Helen
<u>visit a film studio</u>
_____
_____

Paul
_____
_____
_____

Mum
_____
_____

Dad
_____

b ⏵ **12.11** Listen again. Are the sentences true or false?

1 Helen and Paul are brother and sister.
2 Helen is in the USA.
3 She is travelling around by train.
4 She was in San Diego yesterday.
5 Rodeo Drive is famous for its shops.
6 The football game is on Thursday.
7 The next place Helen plans to visit is Las Vegas.
8 Helen is going to phone her parents at the weekend.

c Write a conversation between two friends. One person is going to visit a big city. The other person asks about his or her plans. Remember to say:

• which city he or she's going to visit
• how he or she's going to travel around
• what he or she's going to do and see there.

⊙ Review

1 GRAMMAR

Tick (✓) the sentences that are correct. Correct the mistakes.

1 ✓ Edward isn't going to sleep here tonight. He's at a hotel.
2 ☐ They're going play volleyball. Do you want to watch them?
3 ☐ Are you going to have a bath?
4 ☐ What we are going to do now?
5 ☐ **A** Is he going to work in a bank?
　　B Yes, he's going.
6 ☐ **A** Is she going to go to university?
　　B No, she isn't.
7 ☐ I'm going not to get up early. I'm going to stay in bed until lunchtime!
8 ☐ When I going to see you again?

2 VOCABULARY

Correct the mistakes.

1 See you on the two of March.
　See you on the second of March.
2 They're going to visit Ian on the summer.
3 It's the twelve of August.
4 I'm going to start work in Monday.
5 He was born on the fifteenth of Februry.
6 I've got bread and cheese. I'm going make a sandwich.
7 We could visit Leo and Craig to the party. They love parties!
8 I don't really like sport but I make yoga every day.
9 I want to clean the walls green.
10 Can I do the computer for five minutes? I need to check my emails.

Vox pop video

Unit 1: Hello!

1a ◀ **Hello, my name's Marie. What's your name?**

a Watch video 1a and <u>underline</u> the correct words.

1 *I'm / My name's* Anna.
2 *I'm / My name is* Euan.
3 *I'm / My name is* Nino.
4 *I'm / My name is* Matt.
5 *I'm / My name's* Maibritt.
6 *I'm / My name's* Samantha.
7 *I'm / My name's* Ruby.
8 *I'm / My name's* Colin.
9 *I'm / My name's* Jo.
10 *I'm / My name is* Laurence.
11 *I'm / My name's* Sarah.
12 *I'm / My name's* Jason.
13 *I'm / My name is* Sarah.
14 *I'm / My name's* Laura.
15 *I'm / My name's* Mark.
16 *I'm / My name's* Jenna.
17 *I'm / My name's* Claire.
18 *I'm / My name's* Lauren.

1b ◀ **Are you from England?**

b Watch video 1b and tick (✓) the correct answers.

1 Is Maibritt from England?
   a ☐ Yes
   b ✓ No
2 Is Euan from England?
   a ☐ Yes
   b ☐ No
3 Is Jenna from England?
   a ☐ Yes
   b ☐ No
4 Is Laura from England?
   a ☐ Yes
   b ☐ No
5 Is Ruby from England?
   a ☐ Yes
   b ☐ No

1c ◀ **Are you a student?**

c Watch video 1c. Match the people 1–5 with the sentences a–e.

1 ☐ c ☐ Maibritt
2 ☐ Euan
3 ☐ Jenna
4 ☐ Laura
5 ☐ Ruby

a I am. I study history at the University of York.
b No, I'm a manager.
c No, I'm not. I'm a teacher.
d No, I'm not a student, no. I am an editor.
e Yes, I am.

Unit 2: All about me

2a ◀ **Are you from a city, a town or a village?**

a Watch video 2a and <u>underline</u> the correct words.

1 Sarah's from a *city / town / village*.
2 *It's / It isn't* near London.
3 Anna's from a *big town / small town / big city / small city*.
4 *It's / It isn't* near London.
5 Claire's from a *city / town / village*.
6 *It's / It isn't* near Cambridge.
7 Nino is from a *big town / small town / big city / small city*.
8 *It's / It isn't* in England.

2b ◀ **What's in your bag?**

b Watch video 2b. Match the people 1–4 with the objects a–d.

1 ☐ d ☐ Sarah
2 ☐ Anna
3 ☐ Claire
4 ☐ Nino

a an umbrella, a phone, some keys, an apple
b a bottle of water, a wallet, a phone, an umbrella
c a bottle of water, a photo, a newspaper
d a phone, some keys, a banana, a ticket

2c ◀ **What's your surname?**

c Watch video 2c and tick (✓) the correct answers.

1 Sarah _____
   a ☐ Greaves
   b ✓ Grieves
   c ☐ Greeves

2 Anna _____
   a ☐ Linter
   b ☐ Linta
   c ☐ Linthe

3 Claire _____
   a ☐ Barns
   b ☐ Bahns
   c ☐ Barnes

4 Nino _____
   a ☐ Chelidze
   b ☐ Cheletse
   c ☐ Shelitze

Unit 3: Food and drink

3a ◀ **Do you eat fruit every day?**

a Watch video 3a and <u>underline</u> the correct words.

1 Euan: I *always* / *usually* / *sometimes* eat an apple or a banana at work.
2 Samantha: I *eat* / *don't eat* fruit every day.
3 Samantha: I *like* / *don't like* apples.
4 Colin: I *always* / *usually* / *sometimes* eat fruit once or twice a day.
5 Lauren: I usually have a banana for *breakfast* / *lunch*.

3b ◀ **What time do you eat breakfast?**

b Watch video 3b and tick (✓) the correct answers.

1 Euan: I usually eat breakfast at _____.
   a ✓ 7:00
   b ☐ 7:30
   c ☐ 8:00

2 Euan: I have dinner at _____.
   a ☐ 5:00 or 5:30
   b ☐ 6:00 or 6:30
   c ☐ 7:00 or 7:30

3 Samantha: I have lunch at _____.
   a ☐ 12:00
   b ☐ 1:00
   c ☐ 2:00

4 Samantha: I eat dinner at _____.
   a ☐ 5:30
   b ☐ 6:30
   c ☐ 7:30

5 Colin: I eat lunch at _____.
   a ☐ 12:00
   b ☐ 1:00
   c ☐ 2:00

6 Colin: I eat dinner at _____.
   a ☐ 5:00 or 5:30
   b ☐ 6:30 or 7:00
   c ☐ 5:00 or 7:00

7 Lauren: I have breakfast at _____.
   a ☐ 8:00
   b ☐ 9:00
   c ☐ 10:00

8 Lauren: I eat dinner at _____.
   a ☐ 5:00
   b ☐ 6:00
   c ☐ 7:00

3c ◀ **Do you eat a big meal in the evening?**

c Watch video 3c. Match the people 1–4 with the sentences a–d.

1 ☐ b ☐ Euan
2 ☐ Samantha
3 ☐ Colin
4 ☐ Lauren

a Yes. I usually eat fish and vegetables with rice or pasta.
b Yes. I like Indonesian, Chinese and Italian food.
c Yes. I eat spaghetti or meat and potatoes, or sometimes rice.
d Yes. I like lasagne.

Unit 4: My life and my family

4a ◀ **Where do you study?**

a Watch video 4a. Match 1–4 with a–d to make sentences.

1 ☐ b ☐ Ruby
2 ☐ Lauren
3 ☐ Sarah
4 ☐ Jo

a studies at Bristol University. She studies Languages.
b studies at York University. She studies History.
c studies at Exeter University. She studies German.
d studies at Cambridge University.

4b ◀ **Are you married?**

b Watch video 4b and <u>underline</u> the correct words.

1 Ruby *is* / *isn't* married.
2 Lauren *is* / *isn't* married.
3 Sarah *is* / *isn't* married.
4 Sarah has *one child* / *two children*.
5 Jo *is* / *isn't* married.
6 Jo has *a son* / *a son and a daughter* / *four children*.

4c◀ Do you have brothers and sisters?

c Watch video 4c and <u>underline</u> the correct words.

1 Ruby has four <u>brothers and one sister</u> / sisters and one brother.
2 They are / aren't married.
3 Lauren has one older brother / sister.
4 Lauren's brother is / isn't married.
5 Sarah has two sisters and one brother / two brothers and one sister.
6 They are / aren't married.
7 Jo has one sister / brother.
8 Jo's brother is / isn't married.
9 Jo's brother has one girl and two boys / two girls and one boy.

Unit 5: Places

5a◀ Is there a supermarket near here?

a Watch video 5a and <u>underline</u> the correct words.

1 Jo says there aren't any supermarkets / cafés / <u>hotels</u> near here.
2 Jason says there is / isn't a supermarket near here.
3 Jason says there isn't a hotel / a café near here.
4 Lauren says there's a supermarket and a big café / a small café near here.
5 Lauren says all the hotels / good cafés are in the centre of Cambridge.

5b◀ Are there lots of houses in your street?

b Watch video 5b and tick (✓) the correct answers.

1 There are lots of houses in Jo's street.
  a ☑ True
  b ☐ False
2 There are new and old houses in Jo's street.
  a ☐ True
  b ☐ False
3 There are lots of houses in Jason's street.
  a ☐ True
  b ☐ False
4 There aren't any old houses in Jason's street.
  a ☐ True
  b ☐ False
5 There are lots of houses in Lauren's street.
  a ☐ True
  b ☐ False
6 There aren't any old houses in Lauren's street.
  a ☐ True
  b ☐ False

5c◀ Are there any parks near your house?

c Watch video 5c. Match the people 1–4 with the sentences a–d.

1 ☐ c ☐ Jo
2 ☐ Jason
3 ☐ Maibritt
4 ☐ Lauren

a There isn't a park near the house.
b There's a big park in the next street. People play football and basketball there.
c There's a very large park near my house. I like going there.
d There's a big park. It has a playground and some sports fields.

Unit 6: Work and routines

6a◀ What do you do?

a Watch video 6a and <u>underline</u> the correct words.

1 Maibritt <u>works</u> / doesn't work in Cambridge.
2 Maibritt works / doesn't work long hours.
3 Matt works / doesn't work in Cambridge.
4 Matt works / doesn't work long hours.
5 Mark has / doesn't have a job in a restaurant.
6 Mark works / doesn't work long hours.
7 Laurence works / doesn't work in a factory.
8 Laurence works / doesn't work with computers.

6b◀ When do you usually get up?

b Watch video 6b. Match the people 1–4 with the times a–d.

1 ☐ b ☐ Maibritt
2 ☐ Matt
3 ☐ Mark
4 ☐ Laurence

a 10:00 am
b 6:30 or 7:00 am
c 7:00 am
d 10:00 or 11:00 am

6c◀ When do you usually go to work?

c Watch video 6c and tick (✓) the correct answers.

1 Maibritt goes to work at _____.
  a ☐ 8:00 am
  b ☑ 9:00 am
  c ☐ 10:00 am
2 Matt goes to work at _____.
  a ☐ 11:00 am
  b ☐ 12:00 pm
  c ☐ 1:00 pm
3 Mark goes to work at _____.
  a ☐ 12:00 pm
  b ☐ 1:00 pm
  c ☐ 12:30 pm
4 Laurence goes to work at _____.
  a ☐ 7:00 am
  b ☐ 7:15 am
  c ☐ 7:30 am

Unit 7: Shopping and fashion

7a ◀ **What's your favourite colour?**

a Watch video 7a and tick (✓) the correct answers.

1 Anna's favourite colour is _____.
   a ✓ red
   b ☐ green
   c ☐ yellow

2 Anna often wears _____.
   a ☐ green, grey and brown
   b ☐ purple and blue
   c ☐ green, black and blue

3 Sarah's favourite colour is _____.
   a ☐ grey
   b ☐ purple
   c ☐ brown

4 Sarah often wears _____.
   a ☐ black and white
   b ☐ black and blue
   c ☐ black and purple

5 Claire's favourite colour is _____.
   a ☐ purple
   b ☐ blue
   c ☐ white

6 Claire often wears _____.
   a ☐ grey and purple
   b ☐ green and purple
   c ☐ grey and pale blue

7 Nino likes _____.
   a ☐ grey and blue
   b ☐ white and yellow
   c ☐ green and brown

8 Nino often wears _____.
   a ☐ brown and blue
   b ☐ black and white
   c ☐ red and black

9 Nino _____ wears grey.
   a ☐ always
   b ☐ usually
   c ☐ sometimes

7b ◀ **Which clothes do you often wear together?**

Watch video 7b. Match 1–4 with a–d to make sentences.

1 ☐ d ☐ Anna often wears
2 ☐ Sarah often wears
3 ☐ Claire wears
4 ☐ Nino wears

a trousers, a top and a cardigan or a dress and a cardigan.
b a jumper, a skirt and a pair of boots.
c a skirt and blouse or a dress with high heels.
d jeans and a jumper or a T-shirt.

7c ◀ **Do you like going shopping for clothes?**

c Watch video 7c and underline the correct words.

1 Anna *likes* / *doesn't like* going shopping for clothes.
2 Sarah doesn't like going shopping for clothes because the shops are *expensive* / *busy* / *far away*.
3 Claire goes *to the town centre* / *online* to buy clothes.
4 Nino *likes* / *doesn't like* new clothes.

Unit 8: Past events

8a ◀ **Were you at home last weekend?**

a Watch video 8a and tick (✓) the correct answers.

1 Ruby went to London on Saturday.
   a ✓ True
   b ☐ False

2 She was at home on Sunday.
   a ☐ True
   b ☐ False

3 Euan was at home on Sunday.
   a ☐ True
   b ☐ False

4 He went shopping on Sunday.
   a ☐ True
   b ☐ False

5 Maibritt wasn't at home at the weekend.
   a ☐ True
   b ☐ False

6 Laura was at home at the weekend.
   a ☐ True
   b ☐ False

8b ◀ **Where were you at New Year?**

b Watch video 8b and underline the correct words.

1 Ruby was *at home* / *at a party*.
2 Euan was *at home* / *at a party*.
3 Maibritt was *at home* / *at a party*.
4 Jenna was *at home* / *at a party*.
5 Laura was *at home* / *at a party*.

8c ◀ **What free time activities were popular when you were a child?**

c Watch video 8c. Match the people 1–5 with the free time activities a–e.

1 ☐ e ☐ Ruby
2 ☐ Euan
3 ☐ Maibritt
4 ☐ Jenna
5 ☐ Laura

a doing sport, playing outside in the street, playing with dolls and cars
b doing sport, reading, watching TV, playing music
c football, riding bikes, climbing trees
d playing outside, computer games, riding bikes, football
e reading, playing at the park with friends, computer games

Unit 9: Holidays

9a◀ **Where did you go on holiday last year?**

a Watch video 9a and tick (✓) the correct answers.

1 Euan went to Scotland _____.
  a ☐ by plane
  b ✓ by train

2 Euan _____ in a hotel.
  a ☐ stayed
  b ☐ didn't stay

3 It _____ sunny every day in Scotland.
  a ☐ was
  b ☐ wasn't

4 Samantha went to Turkey _____.
  a ☐ by boat
  b ☐ by plane

5 Samantha _____ in a hotel.
  a ☐ stayed
  b ☐ didn't stay

6 The weather in Turkey was _____ hot.
  a ☐ quite
  b ☐ very

7 Colin _____ to Portugal.
  a ☐ flew
  b ☐ took the train

8 Colin _____ in a hotel.
  a ☐ stayed
  b ☐ didn't stay

9 Lauren _____ in a big hotel in Rome.
  a ☐ stayed
  b ☐ didn't stay

10 It _____ hot and sunny every day in Rome.
  a ☐ was
  b ☐ wasn't

9b◀ **What did you do on holiday last year?**

b Watch video 9b. Match 1–4 with a–d to make sentences.

1 ☐a Euan
2 ☐ Samantha
3 ☐ Colin
4 ☐ Lauren

a visited family and stayed in a caravan.
b walked up mountains, swam in the sea and saw some amazing old buildings.
c saw a lot of old buildings and ate good food.
d went swimming and played tennis.

9c◀ **Did you enjoy your holiday last year?**

c Watch video 9c and underline the correct words.

1 Euan _had_ / _didn't have_ a good time on holiday.
2 Euan's son _liked_ / _didn't like_ staying in a caravan.
3 Samantha _enjoyed_ / _didn't enjoy_ her holiday last year.
4 Samantha _liked_ / _didn't like_ the hot weather.
5 Colin _liked_ / _didn't like_ Portugal very much.
6 Lauren _enjoyed_ / _didn't enjoy_ her holiday last year.
7 Lauren _thought_ / _didn't think_ the holiday was very long.

Unit 10: Here and now

10a◀ **Where do you eat your dinner?**

a Watch video 10a and underline the correct words.

1 Ruby eats dinner in the _living room_ / _dining room_ / _kitchen_.
2 Sarah eats dinner in the _living room_ / _dining room_ / _kitchen_.
3 Jo eats dinner in the _living room_ / _dining room_ / _kitchen_.
4 Lauren eats dinner in the _living room_ / _dining room_ / _kitchen_.

10b◀ **Is there a TV in your home?**

b Watch video 10b and tick (✓) the correct answers.

1 Ruby's family has a small TV.
  a ☐ True
  b ✓ False

2 Sarah has a TV in the dining room.
  a ☐ True
  b ☐ False

3 Jo has a TV in the living room.
  a ☐ True
  b ☐ False

4 Lauren has a new TV in the living room.
  a ☐ True
  b ☐ False

5 Lauren watches TV on the Internet.
  a ☐ True
  b ☐ False

10c◄ Which room do you like best in your home?

c Watch video 10c. Match 1–4 with a–d to make sentences.

1 [b] Ruby likes
2 [ ] Sarah likes
3 [ ] Jo likes
4 [ ] Lauren likes

a her bedroom because all her things are there.
b the kitchen and she spends a lot of time there.
c the living room.
d the living room because it's quite big and there's lots of light.

Unit 11: Achievers

11a◄ Where did you grow up?

a Watch video 11a and underline the correct words.

1 Lauren *grew up* / *didn't grow up* in England.
2 Jason *grew up* / *didn't grow up* in England.
3 Maibritt *grew up* / *didn't grow up* in England.

11b◄ Can you swim?

b Watch video 11b and underline the correct words.

1 Lauren *can swim very well* / *can swim quite well* / *can't swim at all*.
2 Jason *can swim* / *can't swim*.
3 Jo *can swim very well* / *can swim* / *can't swim at all*.
4 Maibritt likes swimming *at the beach* / *in swimming pools*.

11c◄ Can you cook?

c Watch video 11c. Match 1–4 with a–d to make sentences.

1 [b] Lauren
2 [ ] Jason
3 [ ] Jo
4 [ ] Maibritt

a can make cakes, biscuits and bread.
b can cook but not very well.
c can cook traditional English food and curries.
d can cook lasagne.

Unit 12: Plans

12a◄ What are you going to do this evening?

a Watch video 12a and tick (✓) the correct answers.

1 Mark's going to go to _____.
  a [ ] the beach
  b [ ] the cinema
  c [✓] the gym
2 Mark's going to have dinner _____.
  a [ ] at home
  b [ ] at a friend's house
  c [ ] at a restaurant

3 Maibritt's going to _____ and then watch TV.
  a [ ] cook dinner
  b [ ] do yoga
  c [ ] clean her house
4 Laurence is going to _____ some friends.
  a [ ] go to a restaurant with
  b [ ] cook dinner for
  c [ ] do sport with
5 Matt's going to _____ his sister.
  a [ ] have a party for
  b [ ] meet
  c [ ] phone

12b◄ What are you going to do tomorrow?

b Watch video 12b. Match the people 1–4 with their plans a–d.

1 [c] Mark
2 [ ] Maibritt
3 [ ] Laurence
4 [ ] Matt

a I'm going to celebrate my son's birthday.
b I'm going to go for a run.
c I'm going to work.
d I'm going to work.

12c◄ Where are you going to go on your next holiday?

c Watch video 12c and underline the correct words.

1 Mark *is* / *isn't* going to stay in a hotel in Italy.
2 Mark's going to go to the beach and *do a lot of sport* / *go swimming* / *relax*.
3 Maibritt *is* / *isn't* going to stay in a hotel in Denmark.
4 Maibritt's going to visit *her mum* / *lots of museums* / *some friends*.
5 Laurence *is* / *isn't* going to stay in a hotel in France.
6 Laurence is going to *visit some friends* / *go walking* / *do yoga* and have barbecues.
7 Matt's going to stay *in a small hotel* / *on a campsite* / *with his cousin* by the beach.
8 Matt's going to *have barbecues* / *eat at nice restaurants* / *make nice meals*.

Audioscripts

Unit 1

▶ 1.1

1	she	6	not	11	the
2	it	7	from	12	in
3	is	8	I'm	13	hi
4	they're	9	Spain		
5	how	10	thanks		

▶ 1.2

1 **A** This is my friend Mia.
  B Where's she from? Is she Brazilian?
  A No, she isn't. She's from Spain.
2 **C** Who are Bob and Mike? Are they football players?
  D No, they aren't. They're tennis players.
  C Are they British?
  D No, they aren't. They're American.

▶ 1.3

1	Polish	6	Turkish
2	Russian	7	Japanese
3	Chinese	8	Spanish
4	Italian	9	American
5	Brazilian	10	Mexican

▶ 1.4

1 **DEBBIE** Good morning! How are you today?
  AYLA I'm not bad, thanks. And you?
  D I'm OK, thanks.
2 **JENNY** Good afternoon, Dean.
  DEAN Hi Jenny. This is my friend Becky.
  J Hi Becky. How are you?
  BECKY I'm good, thank you. Nice to meet you.

▶ 1.5

CARLA Good afternoon. My name's Carla Watkins.
JAMES Hello, I'm James Hargreaves.
C Nice to meet you, James.
J Nice to meet you too.
C Oh, Greg! This is James Hargreaves from Electric Blue Technology.
GREG Hello, James! How are you?
J I'm fine, thank you. And you?
G I'm good, thanks.

▶ 1.6

1 How are you?
2 I'm fine, thanks.
3 So, this is your office.
4 Good evening!
5 I'm Andy and this is Gaston.
6 Nice to meet you.

▶ 1.7

TOM Good morning. Is this the teachers' room?
ANNE Yes, it is. Are you a new student?
T No, I'm not. I'm a new teacher.
A Oh, are you Tom?
T Yes, Tom Curtis.
A It's nice to meet you, Tom. I'm Anne Walsh, the school manager.
T Nice to meet you, too.
A Where are you from, Tom?
T Edinburgh, in Scotland.
A Really? Edinburgh's a nice city.
T And you?
A I'm from Manchester.
T Oh, right.
A Well, your class is 1A.
T OK.
A This is the class list. It's a small class. There are eight students.
T What countries are they from?
A Let's see. Errrr.... Anna and Olga are from Russia. Lee and Ping are from China. Daniela is from Brazil and Manuel is Spanish.
T And Alim and Fehim. Those are Turkish names. Are they from Turkey?
A Yes, that's right. OK, this is your desk and here are your books ...

Unit 2

▶ 2.1

1	this	4	China	7	hello	10	happy
2	he	5	his	8	what	11	that
3	she	6	her	9	who	12	phone

▶ 2.2

1 I have eighty books.
2 Thirty apples, please.
3 I have six bags.
4 Twelve eggs, please.
5 Do you have fifty tickets?
6 Fourteen bottles of water, please.

▶ 2.3

1	knives	4	newspapers	7	watches
2	villages	5	tickets	8	bottles
3	students	6	books	9	houses

▶ 2.4

A What's your surname?
B It's Milner.
A How do you spell that?
B M-I-L-N-E-R.
A What's your address?
B It's 39 Oak Street, Brighton.
A What's your phone number?
B It's 07896 7421019.

▶ 2.5

A What's your surname?
B It's Gibbins.
A How do you spell that?
B G-I-B-B-I-N-S.
A What's your phone number?
B It's 09745 833081.
A What's your email address?
B It's alice-eight-eight-eight at zipmail dot com.

▶ 2.6

1 How are you?
2 Is it a village?
3 What's your surname?
4 What's your address?
5 Can you spell that?
6 What's the spelling?
7 Are you from a big city?
8 Is this your phone?
9 Where are you from?
10 What's your email address?

▶ 2.7

DARREN I'm Darren. I'm the manager of a TV shop in Manchester. I don't have an office, but I have a chair and a desk in the shop. It's an old desk and it isn't big, but I have a phone, a computer and a newspaper on my desk, and the keys to the shop.
PAULA I'm Paula. I'm a teacher in Washington. I have three desks! One at home, one in the teachers' room at the school, and one in my classroom. I have a laptop and some books on my desk in the teachers' room but I don't have a phone. Today, my bag is on my desk with my umbrella.
JAMIE I'm Jamie. I'm a student in Southampton. I have a desk at school and another desk in my bedroom where I do my homework. I have a computer on my desk at home, and today I also have an apple and a knife, and a glass of water.

Unit 3

▶ 3.1

1 We eat fruit every day.
2 Do you eat bread?
3 They don't eat eggs.
4 **A** Do you like vegetables?
  B No, I don't.
5 Do you like fish?
6 **A** Do you like meat?
  B No, we don't.
7 I don't like rice.
8 **A** Do you like fruit?
  B Yes, I do.

▶ 3.2

DUNCAN Mmm! I like meat! I eat meat every day!
RAJIT Really? I don't eat meat.
D Oh, you don't eat meat. Do you eat fish?
R No, I don't.
D Do you eat eggs?
R Yes, I do. I like eggs.

▶ 3.3

1	my	4	rice	7	I	10	Italy
2	tea	5	milk	8	we	11	meat
3	this	6	is	9	like	12	key

▶ 3.4

1 **A** What fruit do you like?
  B Apples and bananas.
2 **A** Would you like a biscuit with your coffee?
  B No thanks.
3 **A** A tomato is a vegetable.
  B No, it isn't. It's a fruit!
4 **A** We have bread, butter and eggs.
  B Good! An egg sandwich for me, please.
5 **A** A cheese and tomato pizza, please.
  B Certainly.
6 **A** Is this fruit juice?
  B Yes, it's orange juice.

▶ 3.5

1	eight o'clock	5	eleven o'clock
2	half past ten	6	quarter to six
3	quarter past seven	7	quarter past one
4	quarter to one	8	half past one

▶ 3.6

1	morning	6	four
2	afternoon	7	water
3	half	8	class
4	past	9	banana
5	always	10	small

▶ 3.7

WAITRESS Good morning.
NANCY Hello. I'd like a piece of fruit cake, please.
W Certainly. And to drink?
N Can I have a cup of coffee, please?
W Of course. With milk?
N No, thanks.
W Here you are. That's £6.50, please.
N OK. Thank you very much.
W Thank you.

▶ 3.8

WAITER Good afternoon.
SAM Hello. I'd like a cup of tea, please.
W Certainly. And to eat?
S I'd like a cheese sandwich, please.
W With tomato?
S No, thanks. And can I have some chocolate cake and a glass of water too, please?
W Of course! That's £11, please.
S OK. Here you are.
W Thank you.

▶ 3.9

1	a piece of pizza	6	a cup of tea
2	a cup of coffee	7	a glass of milk
3	a glass of water	8	a piece of chocolate cake
4	a piece of cheese		
5	a glass of fruit juice		

▶ 3.10

ANNA What do you want, John?
JOHN A sandwich. What sandwiches do they have?
A They have cheese.
J Oh, I never eat cheese. I don't like it.
A Really? Do you like eggs?
J Oh yes. I like eggs.
A And tomatoes?

J Yes, I eat a lot of tomatoes.

A OK. They have egg and tomato sandwiches. I like those.

J Great. So, two egg and tomato sandwiches.

A Do they have any cake?

J Yes, they have chocolate cake or apple pie with ice cream.

A Well, I don't eat a lot of chocolate, but I like chocolate cake.

J Me, too. And to drink? Tea or coffee? I usually drink tea.

A I don't like hot drinks. Do they have fruit juice?

J Yes, apple juice or orange juice.

A Oh, apple juice. I always have orange juice for breakfast.

J OK. Excuse me …

Unit 4

▶ 4.1

1 Where do you live?
2 Do you speak French?
3 Do you work in a factory?
4 What do you study?
5 Do you go to the gym?
6 When do you have lunch?

▶ 4.2

1 she	4 father	7 they	9 eight
2 that	5 mother	8 the	10 brother
3 right	6 three		

▶ 4.3

CATH Do you have photos of your home?

AMY Yes, I do.

C Can I see them?

A Sure. This is my flat.

C Who's this?

A My brother Harry.

C Great photo!

A Thanks. Here's another picture of my flat.

C It's really nice.

▶ 4.4

JENNY Do you have photos of your family?

SEAN Yes, I do.

J Can I see them?

S Sure. This is my dad and my brother.

J Nice picture!

S And this is me with my mum and my sister.

J They're lovely! Thank you.

▶ 4.5

1 orange	6 Japan
2 question	7 Germany
3 cheap	8 manager
4 page	9 picture
5 child	10 watch

▶ 4.6

BOB Hi, Kerry!

KERRY Hello, Bob. It's so nice to see you! How are you?

I'm fine, thanks. I'm a student at London University now.

Really? What subject do you study?

Business.

Do you like it?

I love it.

And where do you live?

In a house with two other students. And you?

I live in Hong Kong now and I work in an office at the university.

Really? Do you speak Chinese?

Well, I have Chinese classes. My Chinese isn't very good but I speak English at work.

So why are you in England now?

I'm on holiday. I'm here to see my family.

How are your mum and dad?

They're well, thanks. How are your parents?

They're fine. They live in France now, near Paris.

Wow, that's great. Hey, look, is that Ali over there? Ali! … Ali! …

Unit 5

▶ 5.1

1 There's one school here.
2 There are two teachers.
3 There are a few cars.
4 There's a small museum.
5 There are ten families.
6 There's an old hospital.

▶ 5.2

1 few	5 school	9 love
2 butter	6 study	10 who
3 sometimes	7 beautiful	11 funny
4 supermarket	8 pool	12 mother

▶ 5.3

1 **A** Is there a bath in the room?

   B No, there isn't. But there is a shower.

2 **A** There aren't any hotels in this town.

   B Oh.

   A There's a hostel on King Street. It's very good.

   B OK. Thanks.

3 **B** Is there a car park for this hotel?

   A Yes, there is.

   B Are there any empty rooms on the ground floor?

   A No, there aren't. Sorry. There are lots of empty rooms on the top floor.

   B Oh … No thanks.

▶ 5.4

1 bath	5 she	9 museum
2 shower	6 sure	10 shop
3 China	7 six	11 station
4 Russia	8 finish	12 cinema

▶ 5.5

A Excuse me, can you help me?

B Yes, of course.

A Is there a cinema near here?

B No, I'm sorry there aren't any cinemas near here. But there are two in the city centre.

A OK. And is there a museum near here?

B Yes, there is. It's in this street. Just over there.

A Oh yes! Great! Thanks for your help.

B No problem.

▶ 5.6

A Excuse me, can you help me?

B Yes, of course.

A Are there any hotels near here?

B Yes, there are. There's one in the next street.

A Oh, good. And are there any hostels – cheap hostels?

B No, I'm sorry, there aren't.

A OK. Thanks for your help.

B No problem.

▶ 5.7

1 It's a very good hotel.
2 It's so hot today!
3 I'm really sorry.
4 This room's really nice.
5 It's a very big school.
6 This TV is so old!
7 The museum's really boring.
8 The car park's very small.

▶ 5.8

RECEPTIONIST Good morning. Can I help?

MIKE Hi. I'd like a hotel room for the weekend.

R Well, there are lots of different hotels and they have different prices.

M I'd like a room for one person near the beach.

R Hmm, it's summer and there aren't a lot of empty rooms. The Hotel Splendour is near the beach. They have rooms with baths for $160 a day, and breakfast is free. The rooms have TVs and wi-fi, and there's a good restaurant in the hotel.

M It's very expensive and I don't have a lot of money.

R Well, there's the Star Hostel near the station. The rooms are small, but they're clean and a room for one person is only $40.

M That's cheap.

R Yes, it is. There are showers in all the rooms and wi-fi in the café on the ground floor, but you have

to pay for the wi-fi. A lot of backpackers stay there and it's very friendly.

M Is there a restaurant?

R No, there isn't. But there's the café and there are two big supermarkets near the hostel.

M OK.

R Do you want me to phone the hostel?

M Yes, please.

Unit 6

▶ 6.1

1 Hello, I'm Natasha. I'm the hotel receptionist.
2 **A** What's your brother's job?

   B He's a businessman.
3 I'm an IT worker. I work with computers.
4 I'm a taxi driver. I sometimes work at night.
5 I work in this restaurant. I'm a chef.
6 Lionel Messi is a football player.
7 **A** What's your sister's job?

   B She's a waitress.
8 **A** Excuse me! Are you a shop assistant?

   B Yes, I am. Can I help you?

▶ 6.2

1 park	5 sport	9 fruit
2 here	6 work	10 Turkey
3 girl	7 thirty	11 wrong
4 world	8 thirteen	12 university

▶ 6.3

1 **A** Where does Lottie live?

   B In Germany.
2 **A** Does your husband work at night?

   B No, he doesn't.
3 When does Martin get home?
4 What time does she wake up in the morning?
5 When do Kathy and Jim finish work?
6 **A** Does he study English?

   B Yes, he does.

▶ 6.4

1 I wake up at 7:00 am and I get up at 7:15 am.
2 I have breakfast at home.
3 I go to work every day.
4 I start work at 9:00 am and I finish work at 5:30 pm.
5 I arrive home at 6:30 pm.
6 I go to bed at 11:00 pm.

▶ 6.5

1 twenty	3 Spanish	5 fruit
2 breakfast	4 play	6 class

▶ 6.6

DAN Would you like a cup of tea?

EVA Yes, please.

D And would you like a piece of cake?

E No, it's OK, thanks.

D I need to go to the shops for bread.

E I'll come with you.

D That's great, thanks. And I need to make some sandwiches.

E I'll help you.

D Thank you, that's very kind.

▶ 6.7

MEG Would you like a cup of coffee, Rob?

ROB Yes, please.

M And would you like a piece of cake?

R No, I'm fine, thanks – just coffee, please.

M I need to make lunch for Jake and Carrie.

R I'll help you.

M All right. Thanks. We need pizzas.

R I can make pizzas. I make very good pizzas!

M Don't worry. It's OK. The pizzas at the supermarket are fine.

R OK, I'll go to the supermarket.

M Thank you. That's great.

▶ 6.8

1 **A** I need to make dinner for eight people!

   B I can help you.
2 **A** I need to go to the supermarket but I'm really busy.

   B I'll go.
3 **A** Oh no! I haven't got any money with me!

   B I can pay.

4 **A** I can't open this bottle of water!
  B I'll do it.
5 **A** I need to go to the shops. Can you drive me?
  B Sorry, but I'm really busy. Jim can take you.
6 **A** I need some cups. Do you have any cups?
  B No, I don't. I can give you some glasses.

▶ 6.9

PRESENTER Welcome to the show. This week we're talking to people who live and work in Scotland. Today, my guest is 44-year-old Ian Baker. Which part of Scotland are you from, Ian?
IAN I'm from a village near Aberdeen.
P And what do you do?
I Well, I'm a businessman. My wife, Rita, and I have a factory in Aberdeen.
P That's interesting. How many people work there?
I We have 90 workers.
P And what do you make?
I Computers for schools.
P Do you like your work?
I Yes, I do. I work long hours. I start at 7 or 8 in the morning and finish at 7 or 8 in the evening. But my job is never boring. I'm not in my office every day. I go to different places and I meet a lot of people, for example, the teachers and children who use our computers.
P Are all your customers here in the UK?
I No, some customers are here, but schools in South America also buy our computers, so I often fly to Brazil for meetings.
P Are your meetings in English?
I Sometimes, but we usually speak in Portuguese.
P Does your wife go with you?
I No, she works with our customers in the UK and the rest of Europe.
P And how often do you ...

Unit 7

▶ 7.1

1 Do you like these flowers?
2 Do you like those flowers?
3 I'd like that car.
4 I want this car!

▶ 7.2

1 This glass is ten euros fifty.
2 This football is thirty pounds.
3 That guitar is one hundred and twenty-nine dollars ninety-nine.
4 That radio is twenty-four euros seventy-five.
5 Those cups are nine pounds fifty.
6 These plants are three dollars eighty-nine.

▶ 7.3

1	football	6	lamp
2	suitcase	7	guitar
3	glass	8	book
4	bag	9	cup
5	plate	10	plant

▶ 7.4

1 It's Kate's bag.
2 They're Darren's shoes.
3 My friend's jacket's brown.
4 The boys' trousers are new.
5 I never wear jeans.
6 I sometimes wear my sister's clothes.

▶ 7.5

1	jeans	5	nationality	9	Germany
2	large	6	Japanese	10	sure
3	fashion	7	vegetables	11	village
4	shoes	8	shirt	12	shop

▶ 7.6

1 **A** That's £52.95, please.
  B Can I use a card to pay?
  A Yes. Enter your PIN, please.
2 **B** Can I help you?
  B Can I look around?
  A Of course.
3 **A** Here's your receipt.
  B Thanks.
4 **A** How much are these bags?
  B They're £35 each.

5 **A** I'd like that T-shirt, please.
  B Certainly. Here you are.

▶ 7.7

SHOP ASSISTANT Can I help you?
CUSTOMER Yes, how much are these white plates?
SA They're £4 each.
C OK, I'd like four white plates, please.
SA Certainly. That's £16, please.
C Can I use a card to pay?
SA Of course. Enter your PIN, please. OK, here's your receipt. Would you like a bag?
C No, don't worry.
SA OK, here you are.
C Thank you very much.
SA Thank you.

▶ 7.8

1 Here you are.
2 Is it blue or green?
3 Three apples, please.
4 Are you OK?
5 She only wears white.
6 These cups are for me and you.
7 He always wears black.
8 There are two empty bags.

▶ 7.9

PAUL Why do I have to come shopping, Sue? It's so boring.
SUE You know why, Paul. It's your mum's birthday on Sunday. We need to find a present for her.
P That's easy. I always buy a box of chocolates and some flowers from that shop near the station.
S Chocolates and flowers? Those are boring. Let's get something useful for her new flat.
P Oh, right. Well, let's try this store here. They sell lots of nice things.
S OK. Look, these cups and plates are nice. They have pictures of cats on them.
P Mum has a lot of cups. I don't think she needs any more.
S Well, what about a clock? Those clocks over there are nice … Or how about a new lamp? This one is good for reading and your mum loves reading.
P A lamp is a good idea. I don't like the colour though. Do they have any colours?
S I don't think so. They're all brown.
P Oh, right ... Hey, do you like those little red tables over there? I know Mum wants a new table for her laptop.
S Oh, that's a good idea. How much are they?
P £60 each.
S OK, let's get one. And next, we need to go to the card shop and choose a birthday card …

Unit 8

▶ 8.1

A You weren't here on Friday afternoon. Where were you?
B I was with my brothers. We were at a basketball game.
A Oh, was it good?
B No, it wasn't. I don't like basketball.
A Oh. And where were you on Friday evening?
B We were at a party.
A Was it a good party?
B It was OK. The people were really nice, but the music wasn't very good.

▶ 8.2

1 It's January 2016. It was January 2015 a year ago.
2 Today it's Sunday the third of January. It was the second of January yesterday.
3 It's Sunday evening. I was at work from two pm until five thirty pm today. I was at work this afternoon.
4 It's Sunday evening. I was at work from eight thirty am until eleven thirty am today. I was at work this morning.
5 It's Sunday. I was at work from eight pm until eleven thirty pm on Saturday. I was at work last night.
6 It's January 2016. I was in Rome in December 2015. I was in Rome last month.

▶ 8.3

1 James was at home.
2 We were in London.
3 You were at work.
4 My parents were in Italy.
5 The party was fun.
6 The game was exciting.
7 The concert was good.
8 The meetings were interesting.

▶ 8.4

1 I read the newspaper every day.
2 I sometimes watch films on TV.
3 I never go to the cinema.
4 I don't read magazines.
5 I have a shower every evening.
6 I usually listen to the radio in the morning.
7 I often watch football matches on TV.
8 I play computer games every day.
9 I always listen to music in the evening.
10 I always go to parties at the weekend.

▶ 8.5

1	talked	5	played
2	killed	6	watched
3	stayed	7	helped
4	listened	8	arrived

▶ 8.6

ANGELA I went to the beach last week. It was great.
SUZY Oh, let's go to the beach together some time!
A That's a lovely idea.
S We could go this weekend.
A I'm sorry, I'm busy with my family this weekend.
S OK. Shall we go next Saturday?
A I can't go on Saturday but I'm free on Sunday. I can go on Sunday.
S OK, Sunday. Good.
A Great!

▶ 8.7

SAYEED Shall we go for a coffee?
ANYA Coffee? Good idea!
S Great! Let's go now.
A I'm sorry, I can't go now. I have a meeting at ten o'clock.
S OK. We could go at eleven.
A Great! Shall we go to the new Polish café?
S OK, that's a nice idea! See you at eleven.

▶ 8.8

1 Shall we go for a meal tomorrow?
2 That's a lovely idea.
3 Let's go to the cinema next week.
4 That's a great idea.
5 I'm away on Tuesday.
6 That's a nice idea.

▶ 8.9

GRACE Morning, Matt. How was your weekend?
MATT It was good, thanks, Grace. My wife was at work on Saturday, so I was at home with the children. I think they were a bit bored. But we went to a concert in the park yesterday. There were a lot of people.
G Really? How was the concert?
M It was fun. The bands were very good.
G Was it expensive?
M Well, that was the best thing. A family ticket was only £10.00! We had a great day. There was a lot to see and do. Anyway, how was your weekend?
G Oh, it was good. I was in Barcelona.
M Wow! Was it your first visit to Barcelona?
G No, my sister moved there four years ago, and I often visit her.
M Was it hot?
G It wasn't hot, but it wasn't very cold either. On Saturday we went to a restaurant on the beach. We had a lovely meal there, but the restaurant was empty! There weren't any other people.
M What did you do yesterday?
G We went to the National Museum. It was really interesting. We saw so many things.
M How much was it?
G It was free. You don't have to pay to go into some museums on Sunday.

Unit 9

▶ 9.1

1 **A** Our father went to Los Angeles last week. He stayed in a hotel, I think.
 B No, he didn't stay in a hotel. He stayed at a campsite.
2 **A** We visited a lot of museums on holiday.
 B We didn't visit a lot of museums. We visited two museums! That's not a lot!
3 **A** How was the café?
 B I went to the office! I didn't go to a café!
4 **A** They had a car on holiday in France.
 B Well, no, they didn't have a car. They had bikes.
5 **A** I bought a few new clothes yesterday.
 B You didn't buy a few new clothes! You bought a lot of new clothes!
6 **A** I read a lot of books last weekend.
 B You didn't read a lot of books. You read one book! That's all!

▶ 9.2

1	what	5	train	9	watch
2	taxi	6	father	10	want
3	car	7	take	11	camp
4	flat	8	plane	12	garden

▶ 9.3

A What did you do at New Year? Did you go out?
B No, I didn't. I stayed at home.
A Really? Why did you stay at home?
B I wasn't very well.
A Oh, no! Did Jack stay at home?
B No, he didn't. He went into the city.
A Did he see the fireworks?
B Yes, he did.
A What time did he get home?
B I don't know. I was in bed!

▶ 9.4

1 **A** It's −7°C! I don't like winter!
 B Really? I like this season. I like cold weather and I really like snow!
2 **A** It's really windy today.
 B Yes, there's always a lot of wind in the autumn.
3 **A** Look at the rain!
 B I know. It often rains in this country.
4 **A** Did you have good weather on holiday? It was 42°C here.
 B 42°C! No, it wasn't hot but it was warm and sunny every day.

▶ 9.5

1	cloud	5	town	9	doctor
2	hot	6	cold	10	brown
3	snowy	7	phone	11	wrong
4	holiday	8	ago	12	trousers

▶ 9.6

1 **A** Can you go to the shops? We need bread.
 B Sorry, I'm really busy.
 A Oh, OK, I'll do it then.
2 **A** Can you do something for me?
 B Sure, what is it?
 A Could you meet me at the station on Sunday?
 B Yes, certainly.
 A Thanks, that's really kind of you.
3 **A** Can you come to the shops with me today?
 B Sorry, I can't. I'm really busy.
 A Oh, OK. Could you come with me tomorrow?
 B Sure, no problem.
 A Thanks.

▶ 9.7

KERRY Hi, it's Kerry here.
AL Hi Kerry, how are you?
 I'm fine, thanks. Could you do something for me?
 Yes, of course. What is it?
 Can you pick Jenny up from school at four?
 Sure, no problem.
 Thanks, that's really kind of you.
 That's OK. See you later.
 See you.

▶ 9.8

1	lovely	5	autumn	9	restaurant
2	expensive	6	different	10	interesting
3	beautiful	7	museum	11	holiday
4	station	8	cinema	12	campsite

▶ 9.9

Researcher Excuse me, sir. Do you have time to answer a holiday questionnaire?
Man in street Er, yes. OK.
R Thank you. Right, my first question is: When was your last holiday?
M Oh, in autumn. We usually go on holiday in summer, but this year we went in autumn.
R Did you stay in the UK or did you go to another country?
M I went to Faro in Portugal with my wife. The children didn't want to come, so they stayed at home.
R How did you get there?
M Well my wife doesn't like flying, so we went by ship from England to Spain, then we took a train to Faro.
R How long was your holiday?
M Three weeks.
R Did you stay in a hotel?
M No, we didn't. One of our friends has a house near the beach and we stayed there. It was our second holiday there.
R Do you speak Portuguese?
M No, but I learned a few phrases before we left England.
R Why didn't you stay in the UK for your holiday?
M Because Portugal has better weather! England is often cold and rainy in autumn.
R OK, and my next question ...

Unit 10

▶ 10.1

1	bathroom	5	ninth
2	kitchen	6	month
3	picture	7	question
4	chair	8	thirty

▶ 10.2

1 Who are you phoning?
2 We aren't studying.
3 Why is Ryan talking on the phone?
4 I'm not reading this book.
5 Are your friends waiting for the bus?
6 Erica isn't staying at the hotel.

▶ 10.3

ANDY Hi, it's me. Where are you? What are you doing?
TILDA I'm with Jenny and Craig.
A Oh, are you working?
T Yes, we are. Can I have some apple juice, please?
A Apple juice? What are you talking about?
T Sorry, I'm not talking to you. I'm talking to the waiter but he isn't listening.
A Waiter? Is there a waiter at work?
T No, we aren't working in the office. We're in a meeting at a café.
A Oh …

▶ 10.4

1 **A** Where are you? Are you at the airport?
 B No, I'm at the cinema! It's a really good film!
2 **A** Is Pasha at work?
 B No, he's on holiday.
3 **A** You could phone Stella. She's at home.
 B I don't have my phone. It's in the car.
4 **A** Is Allie at school?
 B No, she's in bed.
5 **A** Are you on the bus?
 B No, there aren't any buses. I'm in a taxi.
6 **A** I'm still at the station. The train's late.
 B Oh dear. Can you phone when you're on the train?

▶ 10.5

1	husband	6	ago
2	picture	7	Japanese
3	Brazil	8	hospital
4	daughter	9	computer
5	autumn	10	afternoon

▶ 10.6

A Oh, excuse me!
B Yes? How can I help?
A What time's the next bus to Bath?
B It's at 11:15.
A So it leaves in ten minutes. Is it a direct bus?
B No, you change at Bristol.
A OK, and which bus stop is it?
B Number two, near the ticket office.
A Great! Thanks for your help.

▶ 10.7

A Excuse me.
B Yes? How can I help?
A What time's the next train to Eastbourne?
B The next train leaves in half an hour.
A So at 10:25. Is it a direct train?
B No, you change at Brighton.
A OK, and which platform is it?
B It's platform nine.
A Great! Thanks for your help.
B No problem.

▶ 10.8

1	pair	4	meal	7	here	9	where
2	wear	5	there	8	chair	10	clear
3	we're	6	year				

▶ 10.9

JACK Hi, Mum.
MUM Hello, Jack. Is Dad home yet?
J No, there's no one here except me. Dad phoned from his office half an hour ago. There's a problem so he's working late.
M What are you doing? I can hear music. Are you watching TV?
J No, I'm listening to music and getting ready to go out to the cinema.
M And where's Melinda?
J She's at the sports centre with some of her friends. I think they're playing tennis. What about you?
M I'm at the station with your brother. We're waiting for the train, but there's a problem.
J What do you mean?
M Well the train is late and it's starting to snow now.
J Oh no.
M Tim isn't very happy. He's only wearing his jeans and a jumper. He didn't want to put his coat on when we left the house.
J Can I talk to him?
M Not now. He's in the café – he's buying some hot drinks for us.
J Oh, right.
M Oh, I've got to go! The train is arriving. There are lots of people here on the platform and it's going to be difficult to get a seat. Tim! Tim! Hurry up!

Unit 11

▶ 11.1

A I've got some photos of the party. They're very funny.
B Oh, can I see them?
A Yes, just a minute … OK … My brother's in this picture. He arrived very late.
B Really? Where is he? I can't see him!
A He's there, with the green hat!
B Oh yes! It's a very big hat! Is that you? It's your T-shirt.
A Yes, that's me. I'm with Ian and Debbie. They're really nice.
B And who's that?
A That's Anna-Maria. She's at our house at the moment. She's staying with us.
B Can I meet her?
A Yes, of course. She really wants to meet you!

▶ 11.2

1	work	sport	shirt
2	daughter	thirty	Thursday
3	university	early	near
4	born	first	world
5	people	person	girl
6	Turkish	grow	weren't

▶ 11.3

1 Your pictures are beautiful! You can paint very well.
2 **A** Can you cook?
  B Yes, I can.
3 I like music but I can't dance at all! I'm a terrible dancer!
4 Jenny can speak German very well.
5 **A** Can he run 10 km?
  B No, he can't.
6 They're good swimmers. They can swim very well.

▶ 11.4

1 Can you ride a horse?
2 When did you last paint a picture?
3 How often do you cook a meal for lots of people?
4 You're at a party and you like the music. Do you dance?
5 Did you sing a song yesterday?
6 Can you run 5 km?
7 Do people swim in the sea in your country?
8 How often do you drive a car?

▶ 11.5

1 I can swim.
2 Can you drive?
3 Yes, I can.
4 Jim can't sing.
5 Can he dance?
6 No, he can't.

▶ 11.6

1 **A** What do you think of this room?
  B I don't think grey is a good idea for the walls.
  A Maybe you're right. But I think it's OK with the red bed.
  B I'm not so sure.
2 **A** What did you think of the film?
  B It was terrible!
  C Yes, I agree. It's a really bad film!
  A Really? I don't think so. I liked it.

▶ 11.7

MARK What do you think of my new car?
CARRIE I think it's really nice.
PHILIP I'm not so sure.
C Why not?
P I don't think yellow is a very good colour.
M Maybe you're right.
P Mm.
M What did you think of my old car?

▶ 11.8

1 tourist
2 engineer
3 answer
4 school
5 think
6 listened
7 clocks
8 interesting

stay
enjoy
dance
ask

bank
find
six
paint

▶ 11.9

ALEX What are you doing, Lyn?
LYN Hi Alex. I'm working.
A You're looking at job websites! I hope your manager doesn't see you.
L He isn't in the office.
A Good! Let me see the website. Look! There's a job for a singer on a ship … but you can't sing. Oh, and there's a job for a chef on the same ship. You're a fantastic cook.
L Just one small problem. I can't swim so I don't want to work on a boat.
A Well what about this job as an English teacher in Mexico? You speak Spanish and you love travelling.
L But I can't teach and I don't want to live in a really hot country.
A Oh, right. Well, an IT company in Madrid wants a receptionist.
L I don't want to work in another office.
A How about this job as a tour guide? You take people on bus tours around Oxford.
L Hmm … Sounds interesting. What do they want?
A Someone who knows a lot about Oxford and who can speak English and another language.
L Well I was born in Oxford, so I know a lot about it, but I can't drive.
A You don't drive the bus. You just talk to the passengers.

L Oh right. Well, I'll phone the tour company this afternoon!
A Shhh! Your manager's coming back.

Unit 12

▶ 12.1

1 **A** Is there an email from Stephen? He's going to write to you with information about the boat trip.
  B I don't know. I'm not going to check my emails today or tomorrow.
  A Oh, OK. Well, I'm going to phone him this evening, so I can ask him then.
2 **A** It's the holidays! I'm going to sleep for ten hours every night! I'm going to watch TV every day!
  B Really? That's so boring! My brother and I are going to work on a farm near the mountains. The people there are going to teach us how to ride horses.
  A Hmm, sounds quite interesting. What about your sister?
  B She isn't going to come with us. She wants to stay at home.

▶ 12.2

first
second
third
fourth

fifth
ninth
twelfth
thirteenth

sixteenth
twentieth
twenty-second
thirty-first

▶ 12.3

1 You're going to stay in a hotel.
2 They're going to live in Russia.
3 Anna's going to do her homework.
4 I'm going to check my emails.
5 He's going to listen to music.
6 I'm going to read a book.

▶ 12.4

1 When are we going to meet for coffee?
2 Is he going to have lunch at home?
3 Where are they going to get married?
4 Are you going to drive to the station tomorrow?
5 What's she going to do this evening?
6 How are you going to cook the potatoes?

▶ 12.5

1 **A** What are you going to do this morning?
  B I'm going to clean the house – and you're going to help me!
2 **A** So, is he going to play the piano this evening?
  B Yes, he is. Are you going to listen?
3 **A** What are you and your friends going to do in the holidays?
  B I don't know. We're going to talk about it this afternoon.
4 **A** Where's she going to watch TV?
  B In the living room, I think.
5 When am I going to do all these things on my list?

▶ 12.6

1 wall
2 evening
3 wi-fi
4 visit
5 November
6 volleyball
7 warm
8 drive
9 windy
10 winter
11 weekend
12 invite

▶ 12.7

A Would you like to go to a concert this evening?
B I'd love to, but I have lots of homework for tomorrow.
A You're a good student! Are you free tomorrow night?
B Yes, I am.
A Would you like to go to the cinema?
B Yes, I'd love to. Thank you.

▶ 12.8

A Would you like to come for dinner tomorrow night?
B Sorry, I'm busy then.
A Are you free on Friday?
B No, sorry, I'm busy on Friday too. But Saturday's OK.
A Great! You can come on Saturday.
B Thank you!

▶ 12.9

1 **A** Would you like to come to my party on Saturday?
  B I'd love to come. Thank you.
2 **A** Would you like to go to the cinema on Thursday?
  B Sorry, I'm busy then. But Friday's OK.
  A OK, we can go on Friday.
  B Great!
3 **A** Would you like to come for lunch at the weekend?
  B I'd love to, but I'm away this weekend.
  A Are you free next weekend?
  B Yes, I am.
  A You can come then!
  B Thank you. I'd love to come.

▶ 12.10

1 book
2 pool
3 good
4 school
5 food
6 boots
7 cook
8 look
9 afternoon

▶ 12.11

HELEN Hi, Paul. Can you hear me?
PAUL Hi, Helen. Yes, I can see you and hear you. Where are you now?
H I'm in Los Angeles for three days. I took the bus from San Francisco yesterday.
P What are you going to do there?
H Well, today, after breakfast, I'm going to visit Universal Film Studios and go shopping in Rodeo Drive.
P Wow! Rodeo Drive is expensive.
H I just want to look around. Maybe I'll see someone famous! What about you?
P It's not raining here so I'm going to take the dog for a walk. Then I'm going to have dinner and read a book.
H What about Mum and Dad? Are they at home with you?
P Mum's here but she's in the shower. She's going to to meet some friends later and go to the cinema. Dad went out a few minutes ago. He's going to play tennis with Uncle Mike.
H Oh, right.
P Anyway, tell me the rest of your plans.
H Well, tomorrow morning I'm going to go to the beach and in the afternoon I have a ticket for an American football game. But Thursday is the best day. I'm going to spend the day at Disneyland!
P Wow! It all sounds fantastic.
H It is – America is great! After Los Angeles, I'm going to take a bus to Las Vegas and, after that, Dallas and New Orleans.
P Well, have a good time.
H Thanks, Paul. Tell Mum and Dad I'll phone them tomorrow.

Answer key

Unit 1

1A

1

a 2 I'm 3 aren't 4 We're 5 am I 6 I'm not 7 I am 8 aren't

b 2 We aren't teachers. 3 I'm not from the USA. 4 Are you OK?
5 How are you? 6 Are we in London?

2

a China, Italy, Japan, Spain, Russia, Britain, the USA

b 2 Italy 3 Japan 4 England 5 Russia 6 the USA 7 Spain 8 China

3

a Long sounds: they're, how, I'm, Spain, hi
Short sounds: is, not, from, thanks, the, in

1B

1

a 2 they are 3 Are, they aren't 4 Is she, is 5 isn't

b 2 's/is 3 Is 4 isn't 5 's/is 6 are 7 Are 8 aren't 9 're/are 10 Are
11 aren't 12 're/are

2

a Across: 2 British 5 Russian 7 Polish 9 Australian 10 Japanese
Down: 3 Turkish 4 American 6 Italian 8 Chinese

3

a 2 syllables: Russian, Chinese, Turkish, Spanish
3 syllables: Japanese, Mexican
4 syllables: Italian, Brazilian, American

1C

1

a 2 bad 3 you 4 OK 5 afternoon 6 This 7 are you 8 thank 9 to meet

c 2 My 3 I'm 4 Nice 5 too 6 is 7 Hello 8 thank 9 And 10 thanks

2

a 2 a 3 a 4 b 5 b 6 b

1C Skills for Writing

1

2 b 3 a 4 b 5 b 6 a

2

2 Kadim 3 Turkish. 4 friends 5 Emma. 6 They're 7 Spain 8 Emma
9 American.

2 This is Diana. 3 My teacher is Canadian. 4 Their flat is in London.
5 I'm from Poland. 6 We're American. We're from Seattle.

3

Suggested answer

Hi, my name's Agnessa. I'm from Russia. I'm a student in Warsaw, in Poland.
My friends aren't Russian and they aren't Polish. Lia is Chinese and Kurt is
from Germany. Ana and Lucas are from Brazil.

Reading and listening extension

a 4 b 2 c 1 d 3

True: 2, 4, 5, 7; False: 1, 3, 6, 8

Russia, China, Brazil, Turkey

2 at work 3 Tom 4 Scotland 5 Manchester 6 1A 7 Brazilian 8 Turkish

Review

1

2 **A** Where are you?
3 I'm not a student. I'm a teacher.
4 **A** And who is this?
5 These are my friends. They're American.
6 What's your name?
7 We aren't Italian. We're Mexican.
8 Where is Sue from?

2

2 ✓
3 He's from Russia.
4 ✓
5 We're Brazilian.
6 Are you Spanish?
7 ✓
8 ✓

Unit 2

2A

1

a 2 It's 3 She's 4 They aren't 5 He's 6 isn't 7 It's 8 they are

2

a 2 your 3 his 4 their 5 my 6 her

3

a 2 c 3 a 4 e 5 b 6 d 7 g

b 2 right 3 difficult 4 good 5 happy 6 beautiful 7 easy 8 boring
9 interesting

4

a /h/ sound: he, his, her, hello, who, happy
No /h/ sound: she, China, what, that, phone

2B

1

a 2 tickets 3 watches 4 bottle of water 5 knives 6 countries 7 boys
8 babies 9 villages 10 keys

2

a 2 I have two pens. 3 And do you have a dictionary? 4 Yes, I have a dictionary.
5 Timo, do you have a bottle of water? 6 But I have an apple!

3

a 2 book 3 keys 4 umbrella 5 phone 6 bottle

4

a 2 Thirty 3 six 4 Twelve 5 fifty 6 Fourteen

5

a 1 students, tickets, books
2 newspapers, bottles
3 villages, watches, houses

2C

1

a 2 spell 3 phone number 4 email address 5 first name

b 2 How do you spell that? 3 What's your address?
4 What's your phone number?

d 2 It's 3 How 4 What's 5 It's 6 address 7 It's

2

a 2 ↗ 3 ↘ 4 ↘ 5 ↗ 6 ↘ 7 ↗ 8 ↗ 9 ↘ 10 ↗

2C Skills for Writing

1

a 2 Stewart 3 American 4 745 5 Gem 6 Office 7 9178

2

a 2 F 3 G 4 O 5 X

b 2 spell 3 easy 4 phone 5 address 6 village 7 happy 8 nationality
9 office 10 email

3

a Suggested answer
First name: Sandro
Surname: Alessi
Nationality: Italian
Home address: Flat 5, Old Village Street, Perth
Phone number: 07886 327715
Email: salessi93@powermail.com

Reading and listening extension

1

a 4

b 2 a 3 b 4 b 5 b 6 a 7 a 8 a

2

a 1 one desk 2 three desks 3 two desks

b 1 b 2 c 3 a

c Speaker 1: phone, newspaper, keys
Speaker 2: laptop, handbag, umbrella
Speaker 3: knife, glass of water

Review

1

2 I have three watches.
3 It's a beautiful village.
4 Beijing is a big city.
5 This is Kira and Paul and this is their house.
6 My flat is in an old part of town. It's very small.
7 Where's Anna? This is her bag.
8 Where are the knives?

2

2 small bottles of water
3 thirteen flats
4 an interesting city
5 twelve phones
6 beautiful houses
7 an old umbrella
8 funny books

Unit 3

3A

1

a 2 Do you eat 3 don't eat 4 I don't 5 Do you like 6 don't 7 don't like
8 do

c 2 don't eat 3 you eat 4 don't 5 Do you 6 do 7 like

2

a 2 fruit juice 3 eggs 4 cola 5 fruit 6 milk 7 meat 8 tea 9 bread
10 vegetables 11 rice 12 coffee

b Across: 2 coffee 6 vegetables 7 water 10 eggs 11 cola
Down: 3 fruit 4 fish 5 meat 8 rice 9 tea

3

a 1 tea, we, meat, key
2 this, milk, is, Italy
3 rice, I, like

3B

1

a 2 never eat 3 usually have 4 always have 5 sometimes eat 6 never have

b 2 always eat 3 sometimes eat 4 never have 5 usually have 6 always have

2

a 2 a biscuit 3 tomato 4 An egg sandwich 5 pizza 6 orange

3

a 2 ten 3 past 4 quarter 5 eleven 6 to 7 quarter 8 half

4

a 1 afternoon, half, past, class, banana
2 always, four, water, small

3C

1

a 2 cake 3 are 4 cola 5 sandwich 6 course

b 2 Can I have a cup of coffee, please?
3 No, thanks.
4 OK. Thank you very much.

d 2 eat 3 I'd like 4 can I 5 of water 6 you are

2

a 2 b 3 a 4 b 5 a 6 a 7 b 8 a

3C Skills for Writing

1

a True: 1, 2, 4; False: 3, 5, 6

2

a 2 She is not 3 He is 4 We do not 5 They are not 6 It is

b 1 They're 2 we're, You're not / # You aren't 3 don't 4 we're, It's
5 I'm, He isn't 6 I'm not

3

a Suggested answer

Hi Liam, I'm in New York. It's a great city! I'm very happy. I'm not at work. I'm
in a café with my new friends Rafael and Inez. They're really nice. Speak soon,
Brett

Reading and listening extension

1

a 2 coffee 3 like 4 three 5 don't have 6 evening

b True: 4, 6, 7; False: 1, 2, 3, 5, 8

2

a egg, chocolate, ice cream, tea, fruit juice

b Anna: 2, 5, 7, 8; John: 3, 4, 6

Review

1

2 ✓
3 We sometimes have pizza.
4 ✓
5 ✓
6 I don't like cheese.
7 Do you like meat?
8 They usually eat pizza for lunch.

2

2 ✓
3 We eat rice for lunch every day.
4 ✓
5 I never eat biscuits.
6 We have breakfast at 7:30 am.
7 ✓
8 That sandwich is very big!

Unit 4

4A

1

a 2 Where's your flat? 3 What do you eat for lunch? 4 What are their names?
5 Where do you study? 6 When's she at work?

b 2 do 3 is 4 do 5 are 6 is 7 are 8 do

2

a 2 b 3 a 4 b 5 c 6 a

b Across: 2 go 4 speak 5 teach 6 play
Down: 3 meet 4 study 7 live

3

a 2 Do you <u>speak</u> <u>French</u>? 3 Do you <u>work</u> in a <u>factory</u>? 4 <u>What</u> do you <u>study</u>?
5 Do you <u>go</u> to the <u>gym</u>? 6 <u>When</u> do you <u>have</u> <u>lunch</u>?

4B

1

a 2 teaches 3 lives 4 works 5 studies 6 plays 7 speaks 8 goes

b 2 goes 3 studies 4 has 5 drinks 6 teaches 7 works 8 lives

2

a 27 twenty-seven 45 forty-five 89 eighty-nine 34 thirty-four
98 ninety-eight 66 sixty-six 100 a hundred 72 seventy-two

3

a 2 father 3 mother 4 parents 5 brother 6 daughter 7 son 8 wife
9 sister

4

a 2, 4, 5, 7, 8, 10

4C

1

a 2 I do 3 Can I see 4 This is 5 Who's 6 Great 7 It's

b 2 **SEAN** Yes, I do.
3 **JENNY** Can I see them?
4 **SEAN** Sure. This is my dad and my brother.
5 **JENNY** Nice picture!
6 **SEAN** And this is me with my mum and my sister.
7 **JENNY** They're lovely! Thank you.

2

a 1 question, cheap, child, picture, watch
2 page, Japan, Germany, manager

4C Skills for Writing

1

a 2 big 3 Italy 4 computers 5 is 6 teacher 7 is from 8 are

2

a 2 a 3 a 4 b 5 b 6 b

b 2 They're a lovely family.
3 I don't live here.
4 These are my children Ruben and Cara.
5 I have a small flat in Mexico City.
6 My sister studies English at university.

3

a Suggested answer

This is me with my friends Kerry and Rob. They're married. We're at their
house. It's a new house – it's very big and it's very nice! Kerry teaches young
children and Rob is the manager of a café. He's very funny.

Reading and listening extension

2 c 3 a 4 f 5 b 6 d

2 Tom 3 Anna 4 Daniel 5 Maria 6 Greg 7 Olga 8 Jeff

2 working at a university 3 language lessons 4 a holiday 5 parents

2 Bob 3 Bob 4 Kerry 5 Bob 6 Kerry 7 Kerry 8 Bob's

1 study 2 live 3 in 4 are

Review

He works in Barcelona.
She has two brothers.
What's your name?

5 Her husband goes to work in the evening.
6 My sister studies German.
7 Where do you live?
8 Where are you from?

2

2 Our English class has six women and two men.
3 ✓
4 My sister is twenty-five years old.
5 ✓
6 Their son is thirty-three and their daughter is thirty-five.
7 His mother is a hundred years old.
8 I meet interesting people at work.

Unit 5

5A

1

a 2 There are two teachers. 3 There are a few cars. 4 There's a small museum.
5 There are ten families. 6 There's an old hospital.

c 2 There's 3 There's 4 There are 5 There are 6 There's 7 There are
8 There's

2

a 1 supermarket, school, beautiful, pool, who
2 butter, sometimes, study, love, funny, mother

3

a 2 café 3 school 4 bank 5 restaurant 6 hotel 7 beach 8 park
9 swimming pool 10 station 11 cinema 12 hospital

5B

1

a 2 b 3 b 4 b 5 a 6 a

b 2 isn't 3 is 4 aren't any 5 There's a 6 a 7 there is 8 Are there any
9 aren't 10 are

2

a 2, 4, 5, 6, 8, 10, 11

3

a 2 blanket 3 wi-fi 4 shower 5 room 6 towel 7 car park 8 pillow

b Across: 3 park 4 towel 6 shower
Down: 1 blanket 2 TV 3 pillows 5 wi-fi 7 rooms

5C

1

a 2 there 3 near 4 There's 5 It's

b 2 Is there a cinema near here?
3 OK. And is there a museum near here?
4 Oh yes! Great! Thanks for your help.

d 2 course 3 near 4 next 5 any 6 sorry 7 for 8 No

2

a 2 a 3 a 4 b 5 b 6 b 7 a 8 b

5C Skills for Writing

1

a True: 3, 4, 6, 7; False: 1, 2, 5, 8

2

a 2 a 3 a 4 a 5 a 6 b

b 2 but 3 but 4 but 5 and 6 and 7 but 8 but

3

a Suggested answer

Hi Marco
I'm at the hotel. It's very old but the room is very big (and it has wi-fi). There
isn't a bath but the shower is good and there's lots of hot water. The name of
the hotel is the Beach Hotel but it's near the station and a big cinema. There
aren't any shops but there's a café and two restaurants. The restaurants are
expensive but the café is very cheap and it's good.
See you soon,
Sasha

Reading and listening extension

1

a 3, 4, 7, 8, 9, 10

b 2 Ellen   3 Holly Road   4 High Street   5 Station Road   6 museum
7 ice cream shop   8 offices

2

a True: 1, 4; False: 2, 3

b Hotel Splendour: expensive, free wi-fi, rooms with baths, TVs in rooms, free breakfast
Star Hostel: café, cheap, friendly, small clean rooms, near the station, rooms with showers

c 2 one person   3 beach   4 $160   5 $40   6 ground   7 two   8 The receptionist

Review

1

2   There are two cinemas.
3   ✓
4   ✓
5   No, there aren't.
6   ✓
7   Yes, there is.
8   There aren't any shops here.

2

2   Where's the school?
3   Is there a swimming pool?
4   Can I have a blanket, please?
5   There isn't a pillow on the bed.
6   Where's the hospital?
7   We often go to the beach.
8   Do you have a towel?

Unit 6

6A

1

a 2 don't   3 meet   4 don't   5 doesn't   6 like   7 don't   8 doesn't

b 2 don't teach   3 doesn't like   4 doesn't live   5 don't work   6 doesn't go
7 don't know   8 doesn't speak

2

a 2 factory worker   3 chef   4 waiter   5 football player   6 doctor   7 student
8 shop assistant   9 receptionist   10 office worker

b 2 businessman   3 worker   4 driver   5 chef   6 player   7 waitress   8 assistant

3

a 3, 4, 6, 7, 8, 10, 12

6B

1

a 2 Where does Eduardo work?
3 What time does Richard wake up?
4 How does Amy get home in the evening?
5 Does Carol have breakfast at home?
6 What does your sister do at work?

b 2 Does your husband   3 Martin get   4 does she   5 do Kathy   6 he does

2

a 2 get up   3 go to work   4 start work   5 have lunch   6 finish work
7 have dinner   8 go to bed

b 1 get   2 have   3 go   4 start, finish   5 arrive   6 go

3

a 2 breakfast   3 Spanish   4 play   5 fruit   6 class

6C

1

a 2 would you   3 it's OK   4 come   5 That's   6 I'll   7 that's

c 2 ROB   Yes, please.
3 MEG   And would you like a piece of cake?
4 ROB   No, I'm fine, thanks – just coffee, please.
5 MEG   I need to make lunch for Jake and Carrie.
6 ROB   I'll help you.
7 MEG   All right. Thanks. We need pizzas.
8 ROB   I can make pizzas. I make very good pizzas!
9 MEG   Don't worry. It's OK. The pizzas at the supermarket are fine.
10 ROB   OK, I'll go to the supermarket.
11 MEG   Thank you. That's great.

2

a 2 b   3 a   4 a   5 b   6 b

6C Skills for Writing

1

a 2 a   3 c   4 a   5 c   6 b

2

a 2 They have breakfast at school. They also have lunch at school.
3 I study at university. I am also a waitress.
4 She gets up early. She also goes to bed early.
5 He gets up early because he's a teacher.
6 She sometimes works at night because she's a doctor.

b 2 because   3 also   4 because   5 because   6 also

3

a Suggested answer

My friend Alex is a football player – he plays football every day. He likes his job very much but it isn't easy. He gets up at 6:30 every day and goes to the gym from 7:00 am until 8:00 am. He has breakfast at home. Alex starts football practice at 10:30 am. He finishes work at 12:00 pm and he has lunch at work with the other football players. He also plays football from 2:30 to 4:30 on Saturday afternoons. He doesn't work in the evening. He usually has dinner at home but sometimes he goes to a restaurant. Alex often meets his friends and goes to the cinema.

Reading and listening extension

1

a 1 at the weekend   2 in the morning   3 in the afternoon   4 in the evening
5 at night

b True: 2, 4, 6, 7; False: 1, 3, 5, 8

2

a 2 businessman   3 married   4 Aberdeen   5 Ninety   6 Europe

b 2 doesn't make   3 works   4 doesn't sit   5 meets   6 have   7 speaks
8 doesn't go

Review

1

2   Does he speak English?
3   When does Anna arrive home?
4   Does Pedro like fish?
5   Seb doesn't play tennis.
6   Yes, she does.
7   No, he doesn't.
8   Where does she live?

2

2   ✓
3   She's a taxi driver.
4   I have lunch at work.
5   He's a businessman.
6   ✓
7   ✓
8   I go to bed at 11:00 pm.

Unit 7

7A

1

a 1 these   2 those   3 that   4 this

c 2 These   3 this   4 that   5 this   6 Those   7 that   8 these

2

a 2 plate 3 cup 4 suitcase 5 picture 6 book 7 guitar 8 radio
9 plant 10 football

3

a 2 c 3 b 4 a 5 b 6 a

4

a 2 suitcase 3 glass 4 bag 5 plate 6 lamp 7 guitar 8 book 9 cup
10 plant

7B

1

a 2 They're Darren's shoes. 3 My friend's jacket's brown.
4 The boys' trousers are new. / The boy's trousers are new.
5 I never wear jeans. 6 I sometimes wear my sister's clothes.

c 2 Mehmet's 3 Andrew and Mina's 4 the girls' 5 Sally's 6 the children's

2

a 2 brown 3 yellow 4 white 5 red 6 green 7 black 8 blue

b Across: 2 light 5 red 6 shoes 9 jeans
Down: 3 trousers 4 yellow 7 shirt 8 black

3

a 1 fashion, shoes, nationality, shirt, sure, shop
2 large, Japanese, vegetables, Germany, village

7C

1

a 2 Can I look around? 3 Here's your receipt. 4 How much are these bags?
5 I'd like that T-shirt, please.

c 2 **CUSTOMER** Yes, how much are these white plates?
3 **SHOP ASSISTANT** They're £4 each.
4 **CUSTOMER** OK, I'd like four white plates, please.
5 **SHOP ASSISTANT** Certainly. That's £16, please.
6 **CUSTOMER** Can I use a card to pay?
7 **SHOP ASSISTANT** Of course. Enter your PIN, please. OK, here's your receipt.
Would you like a bag?
8 **CUSTOMER** No, don't worry.
9 **SHOP ASSISTANT** OK, here you are.
10 **CUSTOMER** Thank you very much.
11 **SHOP ASSISTANT** Thank you.

2

2 /w/ 3 /j/ 4 /w/ 5 /j/ 6 /j/ 7 /j/ 8 /w/

7C Skills for Writing

2 C 3 D 4 B 5 A 6 C

2

2 b 3 c 4 c 5 b 6 a 7 c 8 a

2 You're a grandmother!
3 I've got a sandwich, a drink and a banana.
4 These shoes are very expensive!
5 Where is the station?
6 Satako, Kai and Berto are in my class.

Suggested answer

Hi Jason
I saw your advertisement online for things you want to sell. I have a new house
and I need four chairs, two tables and a clock. How much are these things?
Can I pay online by credit card?
I also need two computers. How many computers do you have? How old are
they? How much are they?
Thank you!
Rachel

Reading and listening extension

1

a a 2 b 4 c 3 d 1

b True: 1, 2, 5, 7; False: 3, 4, 6, 8

2

a things for the home

b 4, 5, 7, 9

c 2 useful 3 animals 4 brown 5 colour 6 laptop 7 £60 8 card shop

Review

1

2 These cups are £6.
3 ✓
4 That picture is interesting.
5 I like Martin's shoes.
6 ✓
7 ✓
8 It's Anna and David's computer.

2

2 He has a red guitar.
3 This picture is one hundred and sixty-three pounds.
4 Do you have any black radios?
5 It's a light brown skirt.
6 Where's your green jacket?
7 I have six white shirts.
8 It's a dark grey coat.

Unit 8

8A

1

a 2 Where was Nina this morning? 3 We weren't at the concert last night.
4 They were in Shanghai a week ago. 5 Were you in Moscow last week?
6 Yes, we were. 7 Was Adrian at the meeting this afternoon?
8 No, he wasn't.

b 2 were 3 was 4 were 5 was 6 wasn't 7 were 8 were 9 Was 10 was
11 were 12 wasn't

2

a 2 yesterday 3 this afternoon 4 this morning 5 last night 6 last month

c 2 yesterday 3 this 4 at 5 last night 6 three months ago

3

a 2 We were in London. 3 You were at work. 4 My parents were in Italy.
5 The party was fun. 6 The game was exciting. 7 The concert was good.
8 The meetings were interesting.

8B

1

a Across: 2 saw 4 listened 8 killed 9 read 10 stayed 11 got
Down: 3 went 5 talked 6 had 7 played 10 sat

b 2 watched 3 was 4 killed 5 went 6 saw 7 said 8 talked 9 knew
10 stayed 11 had 12 played

2

a 2 listen to 3 have 4 go 5 have 6 read 7 play 8 watch 9 go

b 2 watch 3 go 4 read 5 have 6 listen to 7 watch 8 play
9 listen to 10 go

3

a 2 /d/ 3 /d/ 4 /d/ 5 /d/ 6 /t/ 7 /t/ 8 /d/

8C

1

a 2 Let's 3 Shall 4 free 5 could

b 2 That's 3 could 4 busy 5 Shall we 6 can't 7 free 8 OK

d 2 **ANYA** Coffee? Good idea!
3 **SAYEED** Great! Let's go now.
4 **ANYA** I'm sorry, I can't go now. I have a meeting at ten o'clock.
5 **SAYEED** OK. We could go at eleven.

6 **ANYA** Great! Shall we go to the new Polish café?
7 **SAYEED** OK, that's a nice idea! See you at eleven.

2

a 2 ↘ 3 ↘ 4 ↘ 5 ↘ 6 ↘

8C Skills for Writing

1

a 2 Oscar 3 Emi 4 Helen 5 Russell 6 Nina

2

a 2 This 3 to say 4 for 5 was 6 I hope 7 Here are 8 wishes

b 2 a 3 f 4 e 5 b 6 c

3

a Suggested answer

Hi Marie
This is a short email to say thank you for lunch on Sunday. The food was great. I liked the fish and the chocolate cake was really nice. It was good to meet your brothers. Andy's very interesting and Martin's very funny! Here are some photos of Martin with the fish and Andy in the garden. I hope we can meet again soon.
Best wishes,
Chris

Reading and listening extension

1

a True: 1, 2, 4; False: 3, 5, 6

b 2 stayed at home 3 tired 4 watched a cookery programme
5 some books 6 dinner 7 four 8 early 9 7:40 10 for a holiday

2

a 2 work 3 a concert 4 the park 5 Barcelona 6 a restaurant
7 the beach 8 a museum

b Grace: 2, 5, 7, 8, 10
Matt: 3, 4, 6, 9

Review

1

2 Emilia wasn't at work yesterday.
3 We were in the USA in 1996.
4 Where were they yesterday?
5 We played tennis.
6 Jessie arrived at nine o'clock.
7 I had breakfast this morning.
8 Carrie went to New York last year.

2

2 I saw Harry last week.
3 ✓
4 ✓
5 They listened to music last night.
6 ✓
7 ✓
8 We went to the cinema yesterday.

Unit 9

9A

1

a 2 didn't stay 3 didn't meet 4 didn't drive 5 didn't go 6 didn't cook

b 2 didn't visit 3 didn't go 4 didn't have 5 didn't buy 6 didn't read

2

a 2 plane 3 bike 4 car 5 underground 6 taxi 7 train 8 bus 9 tram

3

a 1 taxi, flat, camp
2 car, father, garden
3 train, take, plane
4 watch, want

9B

1

a 2 How did you get there? 3 Did you go with a friend? 4 Where did you stay?
5 What time did you get up? 6 Did you buy a lot of things?
7 Did you go to the beach? 8 Did you enjoy the holiday?

b 2 Did you 3 I didn't 4 did you stay 5 Did Jack stay 6 he didn't
7 Did he 8 he did 9 did he get 10 was

2

a

r	a	i	n	y	j	x	l	y	s
z	y	v	p	x	l	z	z	p	p
f	w	a	r	m	j	q	c	k	r
f	y	p	n	b	h	v	o	d	i
y	j	a	q	k	o	x	l	x	n
c	l	u	s	k	t	v	d	d	g
l	b	t	j	z	h	q	t	p	p
o	f	u	q	s	u	m	m	e	r
u	b	m	v	n	k	t	l	v	z
d	q	n	n	j	p	y	f	t	s
y	x	b	v	t	j	z	y	k	n
q	w	i	n	t	e	r	v	q	o
y	p	s	u	n	n	y	z	j	w

b 2 cold 3 snow 4 windy 5 wind 6 rain 7 rains 8 hot 9 warm
10 sunny

3

a 1 snowy, cold, phone, ago
2 town, brown, trousers
3 hot, holiday, doctor, wrong

9C

1

a 1 Oh, OK, I'll do it then.
2 Can you do something for me?
3 Could you meet me at the station on Sunday?
4 Thanks, that's really kind of you.
5 Sorry, I can't. I'm really busy.
6 Sure, no problem.

c 2 **SAL** Hi Kerry, how are you?
3 **KERRY** I'm fine, thanks. Could you do something for me?
4 **SAL** Yes, of course. What is it?
5 **KERRY** Can you pick Jenny up from school at four?
6 **SAL** Sure, no problem.
7 **KERRY** Thanks, that's really kind of you.
8 **SAL** That's OK. See you later.
9 **KERRY** See you.

2

a 2 syllables: station, autumn, different, restaurant, campsite
3 syllables: museum, cinema, interesting, holiday

9C Skills for Writing

1

a 2 Jiang, Fernanda 3 Jiang, Fernanda 4 Liam, Fernanda 5 Jiang, Liam
6 Liam 7 Jiang 8 Jiang, Liam, Fernanda

2

a 2 Then, 3 After that, 4 After that, 5 then, 6 First, 7 Then, 8 After that,

3

a Suggested answer

Last New Year I went to two parties. First, I went to my friend Katherine's house. It wasn't a big party but it was very nice. I didn't stay late because Katherine and her husband have three small children. Next, I drove to a party in a different town. The weather was very bad. It was cold, windy and very rainy. This party was big and exciting. There was lots of good food and music. At 12:00 am my friends and I went into the garden. We saw some fireworks. After that, I went home.

Reading and listening extension

1

a Billy 2   Monica 3   Lee 1

b 2 Monica   3 Billy   4 Lee   5 Billy   6 Monica   7 Monica   8 Lee

2

a 2 doesn't know   3 in the street today   4 man's

b 2 He went on holiday with his wife.
3 ✓
4 They were on holiday for three weeks.
5 They stayed in a house near the beach.
6 It was their second visit to Portugal.
7 ✓
8 ✓

Review

1

2 ✓
3 I didn't see Sabine.
4 What time did you arrive?
5 ✓
6 ✓
7 **B** No, I didn't.
8 ✓

2

2 We took the train to Milan. / We took a train to Milan.
3 We went by plane to Stockholm. / We flew to Stockholm.
4 This is a photo of the snow in the garden.
5 **B** No, we went by bus. / No, we took the bus.
6 It always rains here in the summer. / It's always rainy here in the summer.
7 Did you go by car to Moscow? / Did you drive to Moscow?
8 It was sunny and warm yesterday.

Unit 10

10A

1

a 2 Joe's listening   3 It's raining   4 We're having   5 I'm looking, It's sitting

b 2 's speaking   3 're going   4 'm working   5 's wearing   6 're studying

2

Across: 3 bathroom   4 dining room   6 window   7 living room   8 floor
Down: 2 door   3 bedroom   5 garden   6 wall

3

1 kitchen, picture, chair, question
2 ninth, month, thirty

10B

1

a 2 We aren't studying.   3 Why is Ryan talking on the phone?
4 I'm not reading this book.   5 Are your friends waiting for the bus?
6 Erica isn't staying at the hotel.

b 2 are you working   3 are you talking   4 I'm not talking   5 I'm talking
6 isn't listening   7 aren't working

2

a 2 at   3 at   4 on   5 at   6 on   7 on   8 at   9 in   10 at   11 at   12 at

b 1 **B** at   2 **A** at **B** on   3 **A** at **B** in   4 **A** at **B** in   5 **A** on **B** in   6 **A** at **B** on

3

2 picture   3 Brazil   4 daughter   5 autumn   6 ago   7 Japanese   8 hospital
9 computer   10 afternoon

10C

a 2 office   3 train   4 ten minutes   5 four o'clock   6 stop

b 2 can   3 next   4 at   5 direct   6 change   7 bus stop   8 ticket   9 help
10 problem

c 2 **B** Yes? How can I help?
3 **A** What time's the next train to Eastbourne?

4 **B** The next train leaves in half an hour.
5 **A** So at 10:25. Is it a direct train?
6 **B** No, you change at Brighton.
7 **A** OK, and which platform is it?
8 **B** It's platform 9.
9 **A** Great! Thanks for your help.
10 **B** No problem.

2

a 1 we're, meal, year, here, clear
2 wear, there, chair, where

10C Skills for Writing

1

a True: 2, 5; False: 1, 3, 4, 6

2

a 2 Is the train   3 is he going   4 did you buy   5 does the film start
6 can, get   7 Is it an expensive   8 Does the hotel have

b 2 Is Nick playing on the computer?
3 How many rooms does their flat have?
4 Did the teacher give us any homework yesterday?
5 Where can I buy a bus ticket?
6 Was he at school today?

3

a Suggested answer

Hi Eduardo. Right now I'm going to our English lesson on the bus. Sorry, I can't remember three things. Where is the new classroom? And what time does the lesson start? Did we have any homework? Thanks! See you soon, Carolina

Reading and listening extension

1

a 2 ✓
3 There are four people in the German family.
4 Today is Sunday.
5 ✓
6 Most people in the family are inside now.
7 Anna wants to know what Jenny is doing.

b 2 two   3 house   4 understand   5 Karl   6 playing a game   7 working
8 music

2

a 2 Dad   3 Melinda   4 Mum, Tim / Tim, Mum

b 2 at home   3 listening to music   4 aren't   5 one of her sons   6 coat
7 snow   8 is

Review

1

2 She isn't working today.
3 Are you having lunch?
4 Where's Vicky going?
5 They're sitting in the garden.
6 Is it raining?
7 No, it isn't.
8 Yes, it is.

2

2 ✓
3 I'm in the kitchen.
4 ✓
5 ✓
6 They're in the dining room.
7 ✓
8 George isn't in bed.
9 I'm at the airport.
10 We're in a taxi.

Unit 11

11A

1

a 2 We, us   3 I, her   4 me   5 it   6 He, him   7 you

b 2 They   3 them   4 He   5 he   6 him   7 He   8 It   9 you   10 me
11 They   12 She   13 She   14 us   15 her   16 She   17 you

2

a 2 grow up 3 finish university 4 stop working 5 be born 6 finish school
7 die 8 go to university 9 have a baby

b 2 went to 3 had 4 up 5 school 6 university 7 died 8 stopped 9 got

3

a 2 daughter 3 near 4 born 5 people 6 grow

11B

1

a 2 **A** Can you **B** I can 3 can't 4 can 5 **A** Can he **B** can't 6 can swim very well

c 2 can't swim 3 can read 4 Can, drive 5 can't teach 6 can say
7 can write 8 can't play

2

a 2 e 3 c 4 b 5 g 6 d 7 a 8 h

c Across: 2 played 6 ran 7 cooked 8 painted
Down: 1 swam 3 danced 4 rode 5 drove

3

a 2 b 3 b 4 a 5 a 6 a

11C

1

a 2 right 3 idea 4 nice 5 think 6 agree

b 2 think 3 Maybe you're 4 I 5 so
6 did 7 I agree 8 think so

d 2 think 3 so 4 don't 5 right 6 did

2

a 2 engineer, enjoy 3 answer, dance 4 school, ask 5 think, bank
6 listened, find 7 clocks, six 8 interesting, paint

11C Skills for Writing

1

a 2 a 3 c 4 c 5 a 6 b

2

a 2 They 3 It's 4 It's 5 She's 6 her 7 him 8 we 9 them 10 you

3

a Suggested answer

Hi Alexei
Thanks for your email.

I'm in Manchester at the moment. I'm studying English at a small language
school in the city centre. It's going OK but it's quite difficult for me to learn all
the new words. The pronunciation is also difficult but the lessons are always
fun because the teacher's very good. His name's Jeff and he's from London.

There are nine students in my class. We all come from different countries. We
usually meet for a drink in the evening. It's a good time to practise English.

Goodbye for now.
Write soon!
Damian

Reading and listening extension

1

a 4, 6, 7, 8

b 2 She got a job in London. 3 She finished her university studies.
4 She got married. 5 She had a baby. 6 Her husband died.
7 She went to South Africa. 8 She started teaching.

2

a 2 chef 3 English teacher 4 receptionist 5 tour guide

b 4, 6

c 2 an office 3 Lyn 4 two jobs 5 Spanish 6 hot 7 knows 8 Oxford

Review

1

2 Your dad's an engineer. We could ask him for help.
3 Is your phone new? I like it.

4 Your sister's really nice. How often do you see her?
5 He can ride a horse.
6 Can you drive?
7 I can't sing.
8 **B** Yes, they can.

2

2 I was born in 1995.
3 She died in 2002.
4 I finished university last year.
5 I grew up in a small village in Scotland.
6 My father stopped working last year.
7 She sang a song last week.
8 I drove the car to the station.
9 I ran 10 km last Saturday.
10 We swam in the new swimming pool yesterday.

Unit 12

12A

1

a 2 I'm not going to 3 to phone 4 I'm going to 5 I'm going 6 are going
7 are going 8 She isn't going

c 2 is going to cook 3 am not going to sing 4 is going to do
5 aren't going to stay 6 isn't going to ride 7 am going to have
8 are going to watch 9 aren't going to use

2

a 2 b 3 b 4 c 5 a 6 a 7 b 8 a 9 c 10 c

3

a 2nd second 3rd third 4th fourth 5th fifth 9th ninth 12th twelfth
13th thirteenth 16th sixteenth 20th twentieth 22nd twenty-second
31st thirty-first

4

a 2 They're going to <u>live</u> in <u>Russia</u>.
3 <u>Anna's</u> going to <u>do</u> her <u>homework</u>.
4 I'm going to <u>check</u> my <u>emails</u>.
5 He's going to <u>listen</u> to <u>music</u>.
6 I'm going to <u>read</u> a <u>book</u>.

12B

1

a 2 Is he going to have lunch at home?
3 Where are they going to get married?
4 Are you going to drive to the station tomorrow?
5 What's she going to do this evening?
6 How are you going to cook the potatoes?

c 1 **B** 'm going to clean, 're going to help
2 **A** is he going to play **B** Are you going to listen
3 **A** are you and your friends going to do **B** 're going to talk
4 's she going to watch
5 am I going to do

2

a 2 a 3 e 4 d 5 b 6 g 7 c 8 f

b Across: 5 room 6 use 7 go 8 washing 10 visit 11 make
Down: 2 clean 3 do 4 computer 9 invite

3

a 1 evening, visit, November, volleyball, drive, invite
2 wi-fi, warm, windy, winter, weekend

12C

1

a 2 **B** I'd love to, but I have lots of homework for tomorrow.
3 **A** You're a good student! Are you free tomorrow night?
4 **B** Yes, I am.
5 **A** Would you like to go to the cinema?
6 **B** Yes, I'd love to. Thank you.

c 2 **B** Sorry, I'm busy then.
3 **A** Are you free on Friday?
4 **B** No, sorry, I'm busy on Friday too. But Saturday's OK.
5 **A** Great! You can come on Saturday.
6 **B** Thank you!

e 2 love 3 Would 4 busy 5 OK 6 can 7 come 8 to 9 free 10 Thank

2

a 1 pool, school, food, boots, afternoon
2 good, cook, look

12C Skills for Writing

1

a True: 1, 4, 8; False: 2, 3, 5, 6, 7

2

a 1 Hi Jerry,
2 I'm thinking about having a barbecue in the garden on Saturday evening – chicken, fish, vegetables, things like that. Would you and Ada like to come?
3 Paul's staying with me this week and he can play the guitar really well. We could eat and then sing songs. What do you think? Are you free on Saturday?
4 I hope you can come!
5 Ethan

b 1 Hi Ethan
2 Thank you, that would be lovely. We're busy on Saturday afternoon but we can come in the evening.
3 Is 8:00 OK? Would you like us to bring some food?
4 See you on Saturday!
5 Jerry

3

a Suggested answer

Hi Simon
Thanks, I'd love to come but I'm busy on Saturday. I'm at work in the morning and I'm going to watch my brother in a basketball match in the afternoon. But I'm free on Sunday and Oliver and Jorges are always free on Sundays. What do you think? Is Sunday OK for you?
Martin

Reading and listening extension

1

a 4 b 5 c 3 d 1 e 2

3, 7, 9, 10, 11

2

Helen: see a football match, spend a day at Disneyland
Paul: take the dog for a walk, have dinner, read a book
Mum: meet friends, go to the cinema
Dad: play tennis

True: 1, 2, 5, 7; False: 3, 4, 6, 8

Review

They're going to play volleyball. Do you want to watch them?
✓
What are we going to do now?
Yes, he is.
✓
I'm not going to get up early. I'm going to stay in bed until lunchtime!
When am I going to see you again?

They're going to visit Ian in the summer.
It's the twelfth of August.
I'm going to start work on Monday.
He was born on the fifteenth of February.
I've got bread and cheese. I'm going to make a sandwich.
We could invite Leo and Craig to the party. They love parties!
I don't really like sport but I do yoga every day.
I want to paint the walls green.
Can I use the computer for five minutes? I need to check my emails.

Video exercises

Unit 1

2 I'm 3 My name is 4 I'm 5 I'm 6 My name's 7 My name's
8 I'm 9 My name's 10 I'm 11 I'm 12 My name's 13 My name is
14 My name's 15 My name's 16 My name's 17 My name's
18 My name's

b 2 b 3 a 4 b 5 a

c 2 d 3 e 4 b 5 a

Unit 2

a 2 It isn't 3 big city 4 It isn't 5 village 6 It's 7 big city 8 It isn't

b 2 c 3 b 4 a

c 2 c 3 c 4 a

Unit 3

a 2 eat 3 like 4 usually 5 breakfast

b 2 b 3 b 4 b 5 a 6 c 7 c 8 c

c 2 d 3 c 4 a

Unit 4

a 2 a 3 c 4 d

b 2 isn't 3 is 4 two children 5 is 6 a son

c 2 aren't 3 brother 4 isn't 5 two brothers and one sister 6 are
7 brother 8 is 9 one girl and two boys

Unit 5

a 2 is 3 a hotel 4 a small café 5 hotels

b 2 a 3 a 4 b 5 a 6 b

c 2 a 3 d 4 b

Unit 6

a 2 doesn't work 3 doesn't work 4 works 5 has 6 works 7 doesn't work
8 works

b 2 a 3 d 4 c

c 2 b 3 a 4 c

Unit 7

a 2 c 3 b 4 b 5 a 6 b 7 c 8 a 9 c

b 2 b 3 a 4 c

c 2 busy 3 online 4 likes

Unit 8

a 2 a 3 a 4 b 5 b 6 b

b 2 at home 3 at a party 4 at a party 5 at home

c 2 c 3 a 4 d 5 b

Unit 9

a 2 b 3 b 4 b 5 a 6 b 7 a 8 a 9 b 10 b

b 2 d 3 b 4 c

c 2 liked 3 enjoyed 4 didn't like 5 liked 6 enjoyed 7 didn't think

Unit 10

a 2 dining room 3 kitchen 4 living room

b 2 b 3 a 4 b 5 a

c 2 c 3 d 4 a

Unit 11

a 2 grew up 3 didn't grow up

b 2 can swim 3 can swim 4 in swimming pools

c 2 d 3 c 4 a

Unit 12

a 2 a 3 a 4 b 5 c

b 2 a 3 b 4 d

c 2 relax 3 isn't 4 her mum 5 isn't 6 go walking
7 in a small hotel 8 eat at nice restaurants

Acknowledgements

The authors and publishers acknowledge the following sources of copyright material and are grateful for the permissions granted. While every effort has been made, it has not always been possible to identify the sources of all the material used, or to trace all copyright holders. If any omissions are brought to our notice, we will be happy to include the appropriate acknowledgements on reprinting and in the next update to the digital edition, as applicable.

The publisher has used its best endeavours to ensure that the URLs for external websites referred to in this book are correct and active at the time of going to press. However, the publisher has no responsibility for the websites and can make no guarantee that a site will remain live or that the content is or will remain appropriate.

The publishers are grateful to the following for permission to reproduce copyright photographs and material:

Key: L = left, C = centre, R = right, T = top, B = bottom

p.4(TL): Getty Images/Kevin Dodge; p.5(BL): Getty Images/Paul Crock/Stringer; p.5(T): Shutterstock/Olesia Bilkei; p.6(BR): Shutterstock/Konstantin Chagin; p.7(CR): Shutterstock/William Perugini; p.8(B): Shutterstock/Robert Kneschke; p.9(TL): Shutterstock/gstockstudio; p.9(BR): Shutterstock/Asier Romero; p.10(TL): Shutterstock/Ron Ellis; p.11(BL): Shutterstock/Dmytro Zinkevych; p.12(TR): Getty Images/Alistair Berg; p.13(CL): Shutterstock/Johner Images; p.14(TR): Shutterstock/kaprik; p.14(B): Shutterstock/Neil Mitchell; p.15(BR): Alamy/Barry Diomede; p.18(TL): Alamy/Montgomery Martin; p.18(BR): Shutterstock/Admin5699; p.19(T): Shutterstock/wavebreakmedia; p.20(BL): Shutterstock/Gregory James Van Raalte; p.20(BR): Shutterstock/ARCANGELO; p.21(TL): Shutterstock/CandyBox Images; p.21(BR): Shutterstock/stevemart; p.22(BL): Corbis/Image Source; p.24(T): Getty Images/Brzozowska; p.25(T): Getty Images/Cultura/Innocenti; p.26(B): Shutterstock/Monkey Business Images; p.27(TL): Shutterstock/Monkey Business Images; p.27(CR): Shutterstock/Pecold; p.28(1): Alamy/Andrey Kekyalyaynen; p.28(2): Getty Images/Ken Walsh; p.28(3): Alamy/MBI; p.28(4): Corbis/Duncan Smith; p.28(5): Getty Images/Nico Kai; p.28(6): Getty Images/UpperCut Images; p.28(7): Shutterstock/Pakhnyushchy; p.28(8): Alamy/John Anderson; p.28(9): Shutterstock/Nataliia Budianska; p.28(10): Shutterstock/Kiev.Victor; p.28(11): Shutterstock/andresr; p.28(12): Alamy/Peter D Noyce; p.30(T): Getty Images/Zero Creatives; p.31(BR): Shutterstock/Andrey tiyk; p.32(B): Shutterstock/Jason Batterham; p.33(TL): Shutterstock/Stuart Miles; p.33(BR): Alamy/Image Source; p.34(1): Alamy/Shaun Higson; p.34(2): Shutterstock/michael jung; p.34(3): GettyImages/tunart; p.34(4): Alamy/Cultura Creative; p.34(5): Corbis/Turba; p.34(6): Shutterstock/Tyler Olson; p.34(7): Shutterstock/Monkey Business Images; p.34(8): Shutterstock/Dmitry Kalinovsky; p.34(9): Getty Images/kzenon; p.34(10): Shutterstock/lightwavemedia; p.36(T): Shutterstock/Photographee.eu; p.37(TL): Alamy/

Cultura Creative; p.37(TR): Alamy/Shaun Higson; p.38(B): Shutterstock/wavebreakmedia; p.39(TL): Shutterstock/racorr p.39(BR): Shutterstock/Creativa Images; p.42(B): GettyImag Jana Chytilova; p.43(C): Shutterstock/Ruslan Semichev; p.44(TR): Shutterstock/EPSTOCK; p.44(B): Shutterstock/Darrenp; p.45(CR): Shutterstock/Maria Sbytova; p.45(BL): Alamy/Andrey Kekyalyaynen; p.48(T): Getty Images/Tomas Anderson; p.49(BL): Shutterstock/Christian Bertrand; p.50(E Shutterstock/Brendan Howard; p.50(TR): Shutterstock/Rawp p.51(TL): Shutterstock/Christian Bertrand; p.51(TR): Gareth Boden; p.52(TL): Alamy/Hemis; p.52(1): Alamy/travelbild. com; p.52(2): Shutterstock/Kenishirotie; p.52(3): Alamy/Serg Borisov; p.52(4): Shutterstock/Patryk Kosmider; p.52(5): Shutterstock/Pio3; p.52(6): Shutterstock/guroldinneden; p.5; Shutterstock/ValeStock; p.52(8): Shutterstock/Art Konovalov; p.52(9): Shutterstock/Leonid Andronov; p.53(BR): Shutterstc Ozervoc Alexander; p.54(BL): Getty Images/Elena_Danileiko; p.54(TR): Shutterstock/Maridav; p.55(CL): Getty Images/Gra Shimmin; p.56(TL): Shutterstock/djgis; p.56(TL): Shutterstoc WDG Photo; p.56(TL): Shutterstock/Penka Todorova Vitkova; p.56(B): Shutterstock/Twin Design;p.57(TL): Shutterstock/anyaivanova; p.57(BR): Shutterstock/przis; p.57(BR): Getty Images/Tomas Anderson; p.57(BR): Shutterstock/Michael Warwick; p.58(1): Corbis/68/Ocean; p.58(2): Alamy/IndiaPicture; p.58(3): Alamy/RubberBall; p.58(4): Alamy/MBI; p.58(5): Getty Images/Mark Robert Milan; p.58(6): Get Images/Jupiterimages/Brand X Pictures; p.59(TL): Corbis/Z/BZM Productions/Ocean; p.60(T): Shutterstock/s_oleg; p.62(Shutterstock/Syda Productions; p.63(TL): Shutterstock/Jaimi Duplass; p.63(BR): Getty Images/Michael Heissner; p.64(BL Shutterstock/auremar; p.64(1): Getty Images/Brian McEntire; p.64(2): Shutterstock/I Schmidt; p.64(3): Corbis/Pankaj & In: Shah/Gulf Images; p.64(4): Corbis/Ian Lishman/Juice Images p.64(5): Shutterstock/Mitar Art; p.64(6): Alamy/Paul Baldesa p.64(7): Alamy/Chris Howes/Wild Places Photography; p.64(8 Getty Images/Cultura/Frank & Helena;p.64(9): Getty Images/Image Source; p.65(CL): Getty Images/mediaphotos; p.66(CL Shutterstock/aleksandr hunta; p.66(TR): Getty Images/Andresr; p.67(CR): Alamy/Mark Bolton Photography; p.68(B) Shutterstock/Hank Frentz; p.69(TL): Shutterstock/Artisticco; p.69(BR): Shutterstock/lzf; p.70(TL): Alamy/Art Kowalsky; p.72(B): Shutterstock/Anton Gvozdikov; p.73(BL): Shutterstoc Elzbieta Sekowska; p.74(T): Shutterstock/Gustavo Frazao; p.75(TL): Shutterstock/Ldprod; p.75(BR): Alamy/Inmagine.

Video stills by Rob Maidment and Sharp Focus Productions: p.76, p.80.

The publishers would like to thank the following illustrators: Mark Bird; Mark Duffin; Sally Elford; John Goodwin (Eye Cand Illustration); Dusan Lakicevic (Beehive Illustration); Roger Penwill; Gavin Reece (New Division); Martin Sanders (Beehiv Illustration); Sean 290 (KJA Artists); David Semple; Marie-Eve Tremblay (Colagene); Andrea Turvey (Eye Candy Illustration); Gary Venn (Lemonade Illustration).